United States

HARCOURT BRACE SOCIAL STUDIES

FLORIDA PLANNER

HARCOURT BRACE & COMPANY

Orlando Atlanta Austin Boston San Francisco Chicago Dallas
New York Toronto London

Visit The Learning Site at http://www.hbschool.com

Printed in the United States of America

ISBN 0-15-320142-8

4 5 6 7 8 9 10 021 03 02

CONTENTS

Planning Chart

	FLORIDA GRADE LEVEL EXPECTATIONS	FCAT WRITES	RESOURCES INCLUDING	FCAT PRACTICE
UNIT INTRODUCTION Introduce the Unit Preview Set the Scene with Literature **The People Shall Continue** by Simon Ortiz pp. 38–45	**SS.A.1.2.1.(5.1)** Extends and refines understanding of the effects of individuals, ideas, and decisions on historical events (for example, in the United States). **SS.B.1.2.1.(5.1)** Extends and refines use of maps, globes, charts, graphs, and other geographic tools including map keys and symbols to gather and interpret data and to draw conclusions about physical patterns (for example, in the United States). **SS.B.1.2.2.(5.1)** Knows how regions in the United States are constructed according to physical criteria and human criteria. **SS.D.1.2.2.(5.1)** Understands that scarcity of resources requires choices on many levels, from the individual to societal. **SS.A.1.2.2, SS.A.1.2.3, SS.A.2.2.6, SS.B.2.2.2.(5.1), SS.B.2.2.3.(5.1), SS.B.2.2.4**		► **TECHNOLOGY** Unit 1 Visual Summary Poster Unit 1 Home Letter Unit 1 Text on Tape Audiocassette Video Experiences: Social Studies ► **TIMELINER** ► **THE AMAZING WRITING MACHINE**	

CHAPTER 1

	FLORIDA GRADE LEVEL EXPECTATIONS	FCAT WRITES	RESOURCES INCLUDING	FCAT PRACTICE
LESSON 1 The Search for Early Peoples pp. 47–51	**SS.A.1.2.2.(5.1)** Compares and contrasts primary and secondary accounts of selected historical events (for example, diary entries from a soldier in a Civil War battle and newspaper articles about the same battle). **SS.B.1.2.1.(5.1)** Extends and refines use of maps, globes, charts, graphs, and other geographic tools including map keys and symbols to gather and interpret data and to draw conclusions about physical patterns (for example, in the United States). **SS.B.2.2.1.(5.1)** Understands reasons certain areas of the United States are more densely populated than others. **SS.D.1.2.2.(5.1)** Understands that scarcity of resources requires choices on many levels, from the individual to societal. **SS.A.1.2.1.(5.1), SS.A.1.2.2, SS.A.1.2.3, SS.A.2.2.1, SS.A.2.2.3, SS.A.2.2.5, SS.B.1.2.2, SS.B.1.2.2.(5.1), SS.B.1.2.4, SS.B.2.2.1, SS.B.2.2.2.(5.1)**	**Narrative Writing – Story** Different Indian groups have different stories about the origin of their lands and their people long ago. These stories are called origin stories. Use your imagination and write an origin story explaining how the first people came to the Americas.	Activity Book, p. 1	FCAT Practice Book, p. 1

TIME MANAGEMENT

DAY 1	DAY 2	DAY 3	DAY 4	DAY 5	DAY 6	DAY 7	DAY 8	DAY 9
Unit Introduction	Lesson 1	Skill	Counterpoints	Lesson 2	Skill	Lesson 3	Chapter Review	Chapter Test

	FLORIDA GRADE LEVEL EXPECTATIONS	FCAT WRITES	RESOURCES INCLUDING ▶ TECHNOLOGY	FCAT PRACTICE
SKILL Use a Map to Show Movement pp. 52–53	**SS.B.1.2.1.(5.1)** Extends and refines use of maps, globes, charts, graphs, and other geographic tools including map keys and symbols to gather and interpret data and to draw conclusions about physical patterns (for example, in the United States). **SS.B.1.2.2.(5.1)** Knows how regions in the United States are constructed according to physical criteria and human criteria. **SS.B.2.2.1.(5.1)** Understands reasons certain areas of the United States are more densely populated than others. **SS.B.2.2.2.(5.1)** Understands ways the physical environment supports and constrains human activities in the United States. **SS.A.2.2.2**		Activity Book, p. 2 Transparency 4 ▶ MAPSKILLS	
COUNTERPOINTS How Long Have People Lived in the Americas? pp. 54–55	**SS.A.1.2.2** Uses a variety of methods and sources to understand history (e.g., interpreting diaries, letters, newspapers; and reading maps and graphs) and knows the difference between primary and secondary sources. **SS.A.1.2.2.(5.1)** Compares and contrasts primary and secondary accounts of selected historical events (for example, diary entries from a soldier in a Civil War battle and newspaper articles about the same battle). **SS.A.1.2.3** Understands broad categories of time in years, decades, and centuries.			
LESSON 2 Ancient Indians pp. 56–60 (continued)	**SS.A.2.2.1** Knows the significant scientific and technological achievements of various societies (e.g., the invention of paper in China, Mayan calendars, mummification and the use of cotton in Egypt, astronomical discoveries in the Moslem world, and the Arabic number system). **SS.A.2.2.3** Understands various aspects of family life, structures, and roles in different cultures and in many eras (e.g., pastoral and agrarian families of early civilizations, families of ancient times and medieval families). **SS.B.2.2.2.(5.1)** Understands ways the physical environment supports and constrains human activities in the United States.	**Expository Writing – Report** Over time some American Indians changed their way of life as food gatherers. Instead of hunting, they planted seeds to grow their own food. This was the beginning of agriculture, or farming, and it brought many changes to the Indians' way of life. Write a report explaining how these changes affected the way the Indians lived, worked, and worshipped.	Activity Book, p. 3	FCAT Practice Book, p. 2

Planning Chart

	FLORIDA GRADE LEVEL EXPECTATIONS	FCAT WRITES	RESOURCES INCLUDING ► TECHNOLOGY	FCAT PRACTICE
(continued) **LESSON 2** Ancient Indians pp. 56–60	**SS.D.1.2.2.(5.1)** Understands that scarcity of resources requires choices on many levels, from the individual to societal. **SS.A.1.2.1.(5.1), SS.A.1.2.3, SS.B.2.2.3.(5.1), SS.B.2.2.4**			
SKILL Identify Patterns on Time Lines p. 61	**SS.A.1.2.3** Understands broad categories of time in years, decades, and centuries. **SS.A.1.2.3.(5.1)** Constructs and labels a timeline based on a historical reading (for example, about United States history).		Activity Book, p. 4 Transparency 5 ► TIMELINER	
LESSON 3 Early Civilizations pp. 62–67	**SS.A.2.2.1** Knows the significant scientific and technological achievements of various societies (e.g., the invention of paper in China, Mayan calendars, mummification and the use of cotton in Egypt, astronomical discoveries in the Moslem world, and the Arabic number system). **SS.A.2.2.2** Understands developments in transportation and communication in various societies (e.g., the development of extensive road systems in various cultures, the difficulties of travel and communication encountered by people of various cultures, the origins and changes in writing and how these changes made communication between people more effective). **SS.B.1.2.1.(5.1)** Extends and refines use of maps, globes, charts, graphs, and other geographic tools including map keys and symbols to gather and interpret data and to draw conclusions about physical patterns (for example, in the United States). **SS.B.1.2.2.(5.1)** Knows how regions in the United States are constructed according to physical criteria and human criteria. **SS.A.1.2.1.(5.1), SS.A.1.2.2, SS.A.1.2.3, SS.A.2.2.3, SS.A.2.2.6, SS.A.6.2.6, SS.B.1.2.4, SS.B.2.2.2.(5.1), SS.B.2.2.3.(5.1), SS.B.2.2.4**	**Persuasive Writing – Opinion** The Mound Builders lived in the eastern part of the present-day United States. Imagine that you are an archeologist studying ancient mound-building civilizations. Think about the group of Indians that built the largest and most complex mounds. Then write a paper to persuade fellow archaeologists at your next seminar that the Mississippians were the greatest mound builders of all.	Activity Book, p. 5 ► THE AMAZING WRITING MACHINE	FCAT Practice Book, p. 3
CHAPTER REVIEW pp. 68–69 (continued)	**SS.A.1.2.1.(5.1)** Extends and refines understanding of the effects of individuals, ideas, and decisions on historical events (for example, in the United States). **SS.A.1.2.3.(5.1)** Constructs and labels a timeline based on a historical reading (for example, about United States history).		Activity Book, p. 6 Transparency 6 Assessment Program Chapter 1 Test, pp. 15–18 ► THE AMAZING WRITING MACHINE	

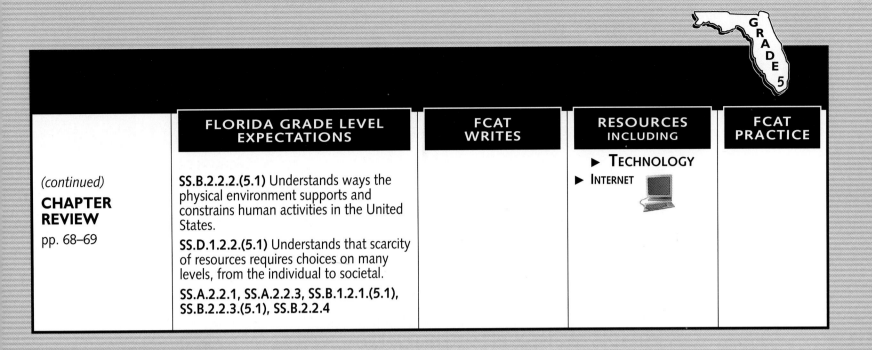

	FLORIDA GRADE LEVEL EXPECTATIONS	FCAT WRITES	RESOURCES INCLUDING ▶ TECHNOLOGY ▶ INTERNET	FCAT PRACTICE
(continued) **CHAPTER REVIEW** pp. 68–69	**SS.B.2.2.2.(5.1)** Understands ways the physical environment supports and constrains human activities in the United States. **SS.D.1.2.2.(5.1)** Understands that scarcity of resources requires choices on many levels, from the individual to societal. **SS.A.2.2.1, SS.A.2.2.3, SS.B.1.2.1.(5.1), SS.B.2.2.3.(5.1), SS.B.2.2.4**			

Teacher's Notes

_____

_____

_____

_____

_____

_____

_____

_____

Planning Chart

	FLORIDA GRADE LEVEL EXPECTATIONS	FCAT WRITES	RESOURCES INCLUDING ► TECHNOLOGY	FCAT PRACTICE
LESSON 1 Northwest Coast pp. 71–75	**SS.A.2.2.2** Understands developments in transportation and communication in various societies (e.g., the development of extensive road systems in various cultures, the difficulties of travel and communication encountered by people of various cultures, the origins and changes in writing and how these changes made communication between people more effective). **SS.A.2.2.3** Understands various aspects of family life, structures, and roles in different cultures and in many eras (e.g., pastoral and agrarian families of early civilizations, families of ancient times and medieval families). **SS.B.1.2.2.(5.1)** Knows how regions in the United States are constructed according to physical criteria and human criteria. **SS.B.2.2.2.(5.1)** Understands ways the physical environment supports and constrains human activities in the United States. SS.A.1.2.2, SS.A.1.2.3, SS.A.2.2.1, SS.A.2.2.6, SS.B.1.2.1.(5.1), SS.B.1.2.4, SS.B.2.2.3.(5.1), SS.B.2.2.4, SS.D.1.2.2.(5.1)	**Narrative Writing – Journal** The Makahs lived in the Northwest Coast area. Imagine that you are a young Makah and have just returned from your first whale hunt. Write a journal entry describing how you prepared for the trip and what happened during the hunt.	Activity Book, p. 7 ► GRAPH LINKS	FCAT Practice Book, p. 4
LESSON 2 Southwest pp. 76–80	**SS.A.2.2.3** Understands various aspects of family life, structures, and roles in different cultures and in many eras (e.g., pastoral and agrarian families of early civilizations, families of ancient times and medieval families). **SS.B.1.2.2.(5.1)** Knows how regions in the United States are constructed according to physical criteria and human criteria. **SS.B.2.2.2.(5.1)** Understands ways the physical environment supports and constrains human activities in the United States.	**Expository Writing – Explanation** Hopi families worked together and cooperated with each other. Write a paragraph that explains the roles of the Hopi men, women, and children. Then share your explanation with your classmates.	Activity Book, p. 8 ► THE AMAZING WRITING MACHINE	FCAT Practice Book, p. 5

(continued)

TIME MANAGEMENT

DAY 1	DAY 2	DAY 3	DAY 4	DAY 5	DAY 6	DAY 7	DAY 8	DAY 9
Lesson 1	Lesson 2	Lesson 3	Lesson 4	Skill	Lesson 5	Chapter Review	Chapter Test	Unit Wrap-Up

	FLORIDA GRADE LEVEL EXPECTATIONS	FCAT WRITES	RESOURCES INCLUDING ► TECHNOLOGY	FCAT PRACTICE
(continued) **LESSON 2** Southwest pp. 76–80	**SS.B.2.2.3.(5.1)** Understands ways human activity has affected the physical environment in various places and times in the United States. **SS.A.1.2.2, SS.A.1.2.3, SS.A.2.2.2, SS.A.2.2.4, SS.A.2.2.6, SS.B.1.2.1.(5.1), SS.B.1.2.4, SS.B.2.2.4**			
LESSON 3 Great Plains pp. 81–84	**SS.A.2.2.3** Understands various aspects of family life, structures, and roles in different cultures and in many eras (e.g., pastoral and agrarian families of early civilizations, families of ancient times and medieval families). **SS.B.2.2.2.(5.1)** Understands ways the physical environment supports and constrains human activities in the United States. **SS.B.2.2.3.(5.1)** Understands ways human activity has affected the physical environment in various places and times in the United States. **SS.D.1.2.2.(5.1)** Understands that scarcity of resources requires choices on many levels, from the individual to societal. **SS.A.1.2.3, SS.A.2.2.1, SS.A.2.2.2, SS.A.2.2.4, SS.B.1.2.2.(5.1), SS.B.1.2.4, SS.B.2.2.4 4**	**Narrative Writing – Poem** Each Indian group that hunted buffalo had special strategies and rituals for the hunt. Think about what it was like to be part of a Mandan hunting party. Then write a poem describing how the Mandan Indians hunted buffalo.	Activity Book, p. 9 Music Audiocassette	FCAT Practice Book, p. 6
LESSON 4 Eastern Woodlands pp. 85–88	**SS.A.2.2.4** Understands the emergence of different laws and systems of government (e.g., monarchy and republic). **SS.B.1.2.2.(5.1)** Knows how regions in the United States are constructed according to physical criteria and human criteria. **SS.B.2.2.2.(5.1)** Understands ways the physical environment supports and constrains human activities in the United States. **SS.D.1.2.2.(5.1)** Understands that scarcity of resources requires choices on many levels, from the individual to societal. **SS.A.1.2.1(5.1), SS.A.1.2.2, SS.A.1.2.3, SS.A.2.2.2, SS.A.2.2.3, SS.A.2.2.6, SS.B.1.2.1.(5.1), SS.B.1.2.4, SS.B.2.2.3.(5.1), SS.B.2.2.4**	**Expository Writing – Description** The Cherokees lived in villages in the Eastern Woodlands long ago. Imagine that you are the Cherokee chief in charge of the game Little War. Think about the rules of the game and the equipment that is used. Then write one or two paragraphs explaining to a person from another tribe how the game is played and why it is important to your people.	Activity Book, p. 10	FCAT Practice Book, p. 7
SKILL Identify Causes and Effects p. 89 *(continued)*	**SS.A.1.2.1.(5.1)** Extends and refines understanding of the effects of individuals, ideas, and decisions on historical events (for example, in the United States).		Activity Book, p. 11 Transparency 7	

Planning Chart

	FLORIDA GRADE LEVEL EXPECTATIONS	FCAT WRITES	RESOURCES INCLUDING ▶ TECHNOLOGY	FCAT PRACTICE
(continued) **SKILL** **Identify Causes and Effects** p. 89	**SS.B.1.2.1.(5.1)** Extends and refines use of maps, globes, charts, graphs, and other geographic tools including map keys and symbols to gather and interpret data and to draw conclusions about physical patterns (for example, in the United States). **SS.B.2.2.2.(5.1)** Understands ways the physical environment supports and constrains human activities in the United States. **SS.B.2.2.3.(5.1)** Understands ways human activity has affected the physical environment in various places and times in the United States. **SS.A.1.2.2, SS.A.2.2.4, SS.B.2.2.4**			
LESSON 5 **Middle America** pp. 90–95	**SS.A.2.2.1** Knows the significant scientific and technological achievements of various societies (e.g., the invention of paper in China, Mayan calendars, mummification and the use of cotton in Egypt, astronomical discoveries in the Moslem world, and the Arabic number system). **SS.A.2.2.3** Understands various aspects of family life, structures, and roles in different cultures and in many eras (e.g., pastoral and agrarian families of early civilizations, families of ancient times and medieval families). **SS.A.2.2.4** Understands the emergence of different laws and systems of government (e.g., monarchy and republic). **SS.B.2.2.3.(5.1)** Understands ways human activity has affected the physical environment in various places and times in the United States. **SS.A.1.2.1.(5.1), SS.A.1.2.2, SS.A.1.2.3, SS.A.2.2.2, SS.A.2.2.6, SS.B.1.2.1.(5.1), SS.B.1.2.2.(5.1), SS.B.1.2.4, SS.B.2.2.2.(5.1), SS.B.2.2.4, SS.D.1.2.2.(5.1)**	**Persuasive Writing – Letter** You are an Aztec builder who is hoping to get the assignment from the emperor to build a new city. What does your city plan look like? What types of buildings will there be? How will the streets and neighborhoods be laid out? Write a letter to the emperor to persuade him that your design for the new city is the best.	Activity Book, p. 12 ▶ THE AMAZING WRITING MACHINE	FCAT Practice Book, p. 8
CHAPTER REVIEW pp. 96–97 *(continued)*	**SS.A.2.2.3** Understands various aspects of family life, structures, and roles in different cultures and in many eras (e.g., pastoral and agrarian families of early civilizations, families of ancient times and medieval families). **SS.A.2.2.4** Understands the emergence of different laws and systems of government (e.g., monarchy and republic).		Activity Book, p. 13 Transparency 8 Assessment Program Chapter 2 Test, pp. 19–22 ▶ THE AMAZING WRITING MACHINE ▶ INTERNET	

	FLORIDA GRADE LEVEL EXPECTATIONS	FCAT WRITES	RESOURCES INCLUDING	FCAT PRACTICE
(continued) **CHAPTER REVIEW** pp. 96–97	**SS.B.1.2.2.(5.1)** Knows how regions in the United States are constructed according to physical criteria and human criteria. **SS.B.2.2.2.(5.1)** Understands ways the physical environment supports and constrains human activities in the United States. **SS.A.1.2.2, SS.A.2.2.2**			
UNIT WRAP-UP Making Social Studies Relevant Visual Summary Unit 1 Review pp. 98–103	**SS.A.1.2.1.(5.1)** Extends and refines understanding of the effects of individuals, ideas, and decisions on historical events (for example, in the United States). **SS.B.1.2.1.(5.1)** Extends and refines use of maps, globes, charts, graphs, and other geographic tools including map keys and symbols to gather and interpret data and to draw conclusions about physical patterns (for example, in the United States). **SS.B.1.2.2.(5.1)** Knows how regions in the United States are constructed according to physical criteria and human criteria. **SS.B.2.2.2.(5.1)** Understands ways the physical environment supports and constrains human activities in the United States. **SS.A.1.2.2, SS.A.1.2.3, SS.A.2.2.1, SS.A.2.2.2, SS.A.2.2.3, SS.A.2.2.4, SS.A.2.2.6, SS.D.1.2.2.(5.1)**		Making Social Studies Relevant Video Unit 1 Visual Summary Poster Game Time! Assessment Program Unit 1 Test, Standard Test, pp. 23–27 Performance Tasks, pp. 28–29 ▶ THE AMAZING WRITING MACHINE ▶ INTERNET	

Teacher's Notes

Planning Chart

	FLORIDA GRADE LEVEL EXPECTATIONS	FCAT WRITES	RESOURCES INCLUDING ▶ TECHNOLOGY	FCAT PRACTICE
UNIT INTRODUCTION Introduce the Unit Preview Set the Scene with Literature 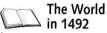 **The World in 1492** by Jean Fritz, Katherine Paterson, Patricia McKissack, Fredrick McKissack, Margaret Mahy, and Jamake Highwater pp. 104–109	**SS.A.1.2.1.(5.1)** Extends and refines understanding of the effects of individuals, ideas, and decisions on historical events (for example, in the United States). **SS.A.1.2.3.(5.1)** Constructs and labels a timeline based on a historical reading (for example, about United States history). **SS.A.4.2.1.(5.1)** Knows selected European explorers and the territories they explored in North America. **SS. A.4.2.1.(5.2)** Understands selected geographic, economic, political, and cultural factors that characterized early exploration of the Americas (for example, impact Native Americans, war between colonial powers, the institution of slavery). SS.A.1.2.2, SS.A.1.2.3, SS.A.2.2.2, SS.A.2.2.6, SS.A.3.2.4, SS.B.1.2.1.(5.1), SS.B.1.2.2.(5.1), SS.B.1.2.3, SS.B.1.2.4, SS.B.2.2.1.(5.1)		▶ **TECHNOLOGY** Unit 2 Visual Summary Poster Unit 2 Home Letter Unit 2 Text on Tape Audiocassette Video Experiences: Social Studies ▶ **TIMELINER**	

CHAPTER 3

	FLORIDA GRADE LEVEL EXPECTATIONS	FCAT WRITES	RESOURCES INCLUDING ▶ TECHNOLOGY	FCAT PRACTICE
LESSON 1 **A Legendary Land** pp. 111–114	**SS.A.2.2.1** Knows the significant scientific and technological achievements of various societies (e.g., the invention of paper in China, Mayan calendars mummification and the use of cotton in Egypt, astronomical discoveries in the Moslem world, and the Arabic number system). **SS.A.4.2.1.(5.1)** Knows selected European explorers and the territories they explored in North America. **SS.B.1.2.1.(5.1)** Extends and refines use of maps, globes, charts, graphs, and other geographic tools including map keys and symbols to gather and interpret data and to draw conclusions about physical patterns (for example, in the United States). **SS.B.1.2.4** Knows how changing transportation and communication technology have affected relationships between locations. SS.A.1.2.1.(5.1), SS.A.1.2.2, SS.A.1.2.3, SS.A.2.2.2, SS.A.2.2.4, SS.A.2.2.6, SS.B.1.2.2.(5.1), SS.B.2.2.3.(5.1), SS.B.2.2.4	**Narrative Writing – Saga** A saga is an adventure story that tells about the brave deeds of people long ago. Imagine that you have just returned from an expedition to Vinland as a member of Leif Eriksson's crew. Write a saga of your trip for the people at home, telling about the adventures you had and the dangers you encountered.	Activity Book, p. 14	FCAT Practice Book, p. 9

TIME MANAGEMENT

DAY 1	DAY 2	DAY 3	DAY 4	DAY 5	DAY 6	DAY 7	DAY 8	DAY 9
Unit Introduction	Lesson 1	Lesson 2	Lesson 3	Skill	Lesson 4	Skill	Chapter Review	Chapter Test

	FLORIDA GRADE LEVEL EXPECTATIONS	FCAT WRITES	RESOURCES INCLUDING	FCAT PRACTICE
LESSON 2 Background to European Exploration pp. 115–119	**SS.A.2.2.6** Knows how trade led to exploration in other regions of the world (e.g., the explorations of Marco Polo and the Vikings). **SS.A.4.2.1.(5.1)** Knows selected European explorers and the territories they explored in North America. **SS.A.4.2.1.(5.2)** Understands selected geographic, economic, political, and cultural factors that characterized early exploration of the Americas (for example, impact on Native Americans, war between colonial powers, the institution of slavery). **SS.B.1.2.4** Knows how changing transportation and communication technology have affected relationships between locations. **SS.A.1.2.1.(5.1), SS.A.1.2.2, SS.A.1.2.3, SS.A.2.2.1, SS.A.2.2.2, SS.A.2.2.4, SS.B.1.2.1(5.1)**	**Persuasive Writing – Request** The Turks have just captured the city of Constantinople and closed the trade routes between Europe and Asia. You are a European sailor who sees this as an opportunity to make your fortune. However, you need help coming up with the money to pay for your venture. Write a letter to the king and queen to persuade them to finance your expedition.	▶ **TECHNOLOGY** Activity Book, p. 15	FCAT Practice Book, p. 10
LESSON 3 Learn History Through Literature "I Columbus My Journal 1492–1493" edited by Peter Roop and Connie Roop pp. 120–123	**SS.A.2.2.4** Understands the emergence of different laws and systems of government. **SS.A.2.2.6** Knows how trade led to exploration in other regions of the world (e.g., the explorations of Marco Polo and the Vikings). **SS.A.4.2.1.(5.1)** Knows selected European explorers and the territories they explored in North America. **SS.A.4.2.1.(5.2)** Understands selected geographic, economic, political, and cultural factors that characterized early exploration of the Americas (for example, impact on Native Americans, war between colonial powers, the institution of slavery). **SS.A.1.2.1.(5.1), SS.A.1.2.2, SS.A.1.2.3, SS.B.1.2.4**	**Expository Writing – Description** One of the rewards Columbus received when he returned to Spain was a personal coat of arms. This coat of arms featured pictures of islands and anchors as symbols of his voyage. Suppose that you were Rodrigo de Triana, the seaman who was the first crew member to sight land in the literature selection, *I Columbus: My Journal*. What would your coat of arms look like? Write a description of it, explaining what the symbols on it represent.	Activity Book, p. 16 ▶ **THE AMAZING WRITING MACHINE**	FCAT Practice Book, p. 11
SKILL Use Latitude and Longitude pp. 124–125 (continued)	**SS.A.1.2.2** Uses a variety of methods and sources to understand history (e.g., interpreting diaries, letters, newspapers; and reading maps and graphs) and knows the difference between primary and secondary sources. **SS.A.4.2.1.(5.1)** Knows selected European explorers and the territories they explored in North America.		Activity Book, p. 17 Transparencies 9A–9B ▶ **MAPSKILLS**	

Planning Chart

	FLORIDA GRADE LEVEL EXPECTATIONS	FCAT WRITES	RESOURCES INCLUDING ▸ TECHNOLOGY	FCAT PRACTICE
(continued) **SKILL** **Use Latitude and Longitude** pp. 124–125	**SS.B.1.2.1.(5.1)** Extends and refines use of maps, globes, charts, graphs, and other geographic tools including map keys and symbols to gather and interpret data and to draw conclusions about physical patterns (for example, in the United States).			
LESSON 4 **Early Voyages of Exploration** pp. 126–130	**SS.A.1.2.2.(5.1)** Compares and contrasts primary and secondary accounts of selected historical events (for example, diary entries from a soldier in a Civil War battle and newspaper articles about the same battle). **SS.A.4.2.1.(5.1)** Knows selected European explorers and the territories they explored in North America. **SS.A.4.2.1.(5.2)** Understands selected geographic, economic, political, and cultural factors that characterized early exploration of the Americas (for example, impact on Native Americans, war between colonial powers, the institution of slavery). **SS.D.1.2.2.(5.1)** Understands that scarcity of resources requires choices on many levels, from the individual to the societal. **SS.A.1.2.1.(5.1), SS.A.1.2.2, SS.A.1.2.3, SS.A.2.2.1, SS.A.2.2.2, SS.A.2.2.6, SS.B.1.2.1.(5.1), SS.B.1.2.2.(5.1)**	**Expository Writing – Explanation** Until his death, Christopher Columbus believed that he had found a new water route to Asia. Other explorers disagreed with him. What was Amerigo Vespucci's conclusion? What was his evidence? Write a paper titled "Columbus Did NOT Reach the Americas" by Vasco Nuñez de Balboa.	Activity Book, p. 18 ▸ THE AMAZING WRITING MACHINE ▸ GEOGRAPHY SEARCH	FCAT Practice Book, p. 12
SKILL **Form a Logical Conclusion** p. 131	**SS.A.2.2.1** Knows the significant scientific and technological achievements of various societies (e.g., the invention of paper in China, Mayan calendars mummification and the use of cotton in Egypt, astronomical discoveries in the Moslem world, and the Arabic number system). **SS.A.2.2.2** Understands developments in transportation and communication in various societies (e.g., the development of extensive road systems in various cultures, the difficulties of travel and communication encountered by people of various cultures, the origins and changes in writing and how these changes made communication between people more effective). **SS.A.4.2.1.(5.1)** Knows selected European explorers and the territories they explored in North America. **SS.B.1.2.2.(5.1)** Knows how regions in the United States are constructed according to physical criteria and human criteria.		Activity Book, p. 19 Transparency 10	

	FLORIDA GRADE LEVEL EXPECTATIONS	FCAT WRITES	RESOURCES INCLUDING	FCAT PRACTICE
CHAPTER REVIEW pp. 132–133	**SS.A.4.2.1.(5.1)** Knows selected European explorers and the territories they explored in North America. **SS.A.4.2.1.(5.2)** Understands selected geographic, economic, political, and cultural factors that characterized early exploration of the Americas (for example, impact on Native Americans, war between colonial powers, the institution of slavery). **SS.B.1.2.1.(5.1)** Extends and refines use of maps, globes, charts, graphs, and other geographic tools including map keys and symbols to gather and interpret data and to draw conclusions about physical patterns (for example, in the United States). **SS.B.1.2.2.(5.1)** Knows how regions in the United States are constructed according to physical criteria and human criteria. **SS.A.1.2.1.(5.1), SS.A.1.2.3, SS.A.2.2.1, SS.A.2.2.2, SS.A.2.2.6**		▶ **TECHNOLOGY** Activity Book, p. 20 Transparency 11 Assessment Program Chapter 3 Test, pp. 31–34 ▶ **THE AMAZING WRITING MACHINE** ▶ **TIMELINER** ▶ **INTERNET**	

Teacher's Notes

_____

_____

_____

_____

_____

_____

_____

Planning Chart

	FLORIDA GRADE LEVEL EXPECTATIONS	FCAT WRITES	RESOURCES INCLUDING ▶ TECHNOLOGY	FCAT PRACTICE
LESSON 1 Conquest of the Aztecs and Incas pp. 135–138	**SS.A.2.2.4** Understands the emergence of different laws and systems of government. **SS.A.4.2.1.(5.1)** Knows selected European explorers and the territories they explored in North America. **SS.A.4.2.1.(5.2)** Understands selected geographic, economic, political, and cultural factors that characterized early exploration of the Americas (for example, impact on Native Americans, war between colonial powers, the institution of slavery). **SS.B.1.2.2.(5.1)** Knows how regions in the United States are constructed according to physical criteria and human criteria. **SS.A.1.2.1.(5.1), SS.A.1.2.2, SS.A.1.2.3, SS.A.2.2.1, SS.A.2.2.5, SS.B.1.2.1.(5.1)**	**Expository Writing – Explanation** Spanish conquistadors were able to conquer advanced societies such as the Aztecs and the Incas. Write a paragraph for a younger student, explaining how the conquistadors were able to do this.	Activity Book, p. 21 ▶ **GRAPH LINKS** ▶ **THE AMAZING WRITING MACHINE**	FCAT Practice Book, p. 13
LESSON 2 The Search for Gold and Riches pp. 139–142	**SS.A.4.2.1.(5.1)** Knows selected European explorers and the territories they explored in North America. **SS.A.4.2.1.(5.2)** Understands selected geographic, economic, political, and cultural factors that characterized early exploration of the Americas (for example, impact on Native Americans, war between colonial powers, the institution of slavery). **SS.A.4.2.2.(5.1)** Knows significant events in the colonization of North America, including but not limited to the Jamestown and Plymouth settlements, and the formation of the thirteen original colonies. **SS.B.1.2.1.(5.1)** Extends and refines use of maps, globes, charts, graphs, and other geographic tools including map keys and symbols to gather and interpret data and to draw conclusions about physical patterns (for example, in the United States). **SS.A.1.2.1.(5.1), SS.A.1.2.2, SS.A.1.2.3, SS.A.2.2.2, SS.A.2.2.4, SS.A.2.2.6, SS.B.1.2.2.(5.1)**	**Narrative Writing – Story** The Fountain of Youth was said to make old people young again. Imagine that Juan Ponce de León did find the Fountain of Youth. Write a story telling what happened.	Activity Book, p. 22 Desk Maps Music Audiocassette	FCAT Practice Book, p. 14

TIME MANAGEMENT

DAY 1	DAY 2	DAY 3	DAY 4	DAY 5	DAY 6	DAY 7	DAY 8	DAY 9
Lesson 1	Lesson 2	Lesson 3	Lesson 4	Lesson 5	Skill	Chapter Review	Chapter Test	Unit Wrap-Up

	FLORIDA GRADE LEVEL EXPECTATIONS	FCAT WRITES	RESOURCES INCLUDING	FCAT PRACTICE
LESSON 3 New People in the Americas pp. 143–146	**SS.A.4.2.1.(5.1)** Knows selected European explorers and the territories they explored in North America. **SS.A.4.2.1.(5.2)** Understands selected geographic, economic, political, and cultural factors that characterized early exploration of the Americas (for example, impact on Native Americans, war between colonial powers, the institution of slavery). **SS.A.4.2.2.(5.2)** Understands selected aspects of everyday life in Colonial America (for example, impact of religions, types of work, use of land, leisure activities, relations with Native Americans, slavery). **SS.D.1.2.2.(5.1)** Understands that scarcity of resources requires choices on many levels, from the individual to societal. SS.A.1.2.1.(5.1), SS.A.1.2.2, SS.A.1.2.3, SS.A.2.2.6, SS.A.4.2.2.(5.1), SS.B.1.2.1.(5.1), SS.B.1.2.2.(5.1), SS.B.2.2.3.(5.1), SS.B.2.2.4	**Expository Writing – Explanation** The colonists in New Spain made the Indian people their slaves. Bartolomé Las Casas worked to get laws passed that protected the Indians. Write a paragraph explaining why he thought the Indian workers should be protected.	► **TECHNOLOGY** Activity Book, p. 23 ► THE AMAZING WRITING MACHINE ► MAPSKILLS	FCAT Practice Book, p. 15
LESSON 4 Encounters with the French and Dutch pp. 147–150	**SS.A.4.2.1.(5.1)** Knows selected European explorers and the territories they explored in North America. **SS.A.4.2.1.(5.2)** Understands selected geographic, economic, political, and cultural factors that characterized early exploration of the Americas (for example, impact on Native Americans, war between colonial powers, the institution of slavery). **SS.A.4.2.2.(5.1)** Knows significant events in the colonization of North America, including but not limited to the Jamestown and Plymouth settlements, and the formation of the thirteen original colonies. **SS.D.1.2.1.(5.1)** Knows examples from United Sates history that demonstrate an understanding that all decisions involve opportunity costs and that making effective decisions involves considering the costs and the benefits associated with alternative choices. SS.A.1.2.1.(5.1), SS.A.1.2.2, SS.A.1.2.3, SS.A.2.2.2, SS.A.2.2.6, SS.A.4.2.2.(5.2), SS.B.1.2.1.(5.1), SS.B.1.2.2.(5.1), SS.B.2.2.3.(5.1), SS.D.1.2.2.(5.1), SS.D.2.2.1.(5.1)	**Persuasive Writing – Speech** Imagine that you are at a meeting of the Iroquois Council. Some members are concerned with the effect that trade with the French is having on the Iroquois way of life. You, on the other hand, believe that trading is good for your tribe. What argument would you present to the council in support of continuing trade with the Europeans? Write a speech to give to the council supporting your views.	Activity Book, p. 24 Desk Maps	FCAT Practice Book, p. 16

Planning Chart

	FLORIDA GRADE LEVEL EXPECTATIONS	FCAT WRITES	RESOURCES INCLUDING	FCAT PRACTICE
LESSON 5 The English in the Americas pp. 151–156	**SS.A.4.2.2.(5.1)** Knows significant events in the colonization of North America, including but not limited to the Jamestown and Plymouth settlements, and the formation of the thirteen original colonies. **SS.A.4.2.2.(5.2)** Understands selected aspects of everyday life in Colonial America (for example, impact of religions, types of work, use of land, leisure activities, relations with Native Americans, slavery). **SS.A.4.2.4.(5.1)** Knows the history of events and the historic figures responsible for historical documents important to the founding of the United States (including but not limited to the Declaration of Independence, the United States Constitution, the Bill of Rights, the Federalist Papers). **SS.D.1.2.2.(5.1)** Understands that scarcity of resources requires choices on many levels, from the individual to societal. **SS.A.1.2.1.(5.1), SS.A.3.2.3, SS.A.4.2.1.(5.1), SS.A.4.2.1.(5.2), SS.A.4.2.4.(5.2), SS.B.1.2.1.(5.1), SS.B.1.2.2.(5.1), SS.B.2.2.1.(5.1), SS.B.2.2.2.(5.1), SS.B.2.2.3.(5.1), SS.D.1.2.1.(5.1)**	**Narrative Writing – Journal** Sir Walter Raleigh chose John White to settle England's first colony in North America, Roanoke Island. Imagine that you are John White and have just returned to the Roanoke colony after a three-year absence to find all of your friends and family members missing. Write an entry in your journal, describing what you saw and your theory about what happened to the lost colonists.	▶ **TECHNOLOGY** Activity Book, p. 25 ▶ **DECISIONS, DECISIONS** ▶ **THE AMAZING WRITING MACHINE**	FCAT Practice Book, p. 17
SKILL Read a Vertical Time Line p. 157	**SS.A.1.2.1.(5.1)** Extends and refines understanding of the effects of individuals, ideas, and decisions on historical events (for example, in the United States). **SS.A.1.2.3.(5.1)** Constructs and labels a timeline based on a historical reading (for example, about United States history). **SS.A.4.2.2.(5.1)** Knows significant events in the colonization of North America, including but not limited to the Jamestown and Plymouth settlements, and the formation of the thirteen original colonies. **SS.B.1.2.2.(5.1)** Knows how regions in the United States are constructed according to physical criteria and human criteria. **SS.A.1.2.3, SS.A.3.2.4, SS.B.1.2.1.(5.1)**		Activity Book, pp. 26–27 Transparency 12 ▶ **TIMELINER**	

	FLORIDA GRADE LEVEL EXPECTATIONS	FCAT WRITES	RESOURCES INCLUDING	FCAT PRACTICE
CHAPTER REVIEW pp. 158–159	**SS.A.4.2.1.(5.1)** Knows selected European explorers and the territories they explored in North America. **SS.A.4.2.1.(5.2)** Understands selected geographic, economic, political, and cultural factors that characterized early exploration of the Americas (for example, impact on Native Americans, war between colonial powers, the institution of slavery). **SS.A.4.2.2.(5.1)** Knows significant events in the colonization of North America, including but not limited to the Jamestown and Plymouth settlements, and the formation of the thirteen original colonies. **SS.A.4.2.2.(5.2)** Understands selected aspects of everyday life in Colonial America (for example, impact of religions, types of work, use of land, leisure activities, relations with Native Americans, slavery). **SS.A.1.2.1.(5.1), SS.A.1.2.3, SS.A.2.2.2, SS.A.2.2.4, SS.A.2.2.6, SS.A.3.2.1, SS.A.3.2.4, SS.B.1.2.1.(5.1) SS.B.2.2.2.(5.1), SS.B.2.2.3.(5.1), SS.D.1.2.2.(5.1)**		Activity Book, p. 28 Transparency 13 Assessment Program Chapter 4 Test, pp. 35–38 ▶ THE AMAZING WRITING MACHINE ▶ TIMELINER ▶ INTERNET	
UNIT WRAP-UP Making Social Studies Relevant Visual Summary Unit 2 Review pp. 160–165	**SS.A.4.2.1.(5.1)** Knows selected European explorers and the territories they explored in North America. **SS.A.4.2.1.(5.2)** Understands selected geographic, economic, political, and cultural factors that characterized early exploration of the Americas (for example, impact on Native Americans, war between colonial powers, the institution of slavery). **SS.A.4.2.2.(5.1)** Knows significant events in the colonization of North America, including but not limited to the Jamestown and Plymouth settlements, and the formation of the thirteen original colonies. **SS.A.4.2.2.(5.2)** Understands selected aspects of everyday life in Colonial America (for example, impact of religions, types of work, use of land, leisure activities, relations with Native Americans, slavery). **SS.A.1.2.1.(5.1), SS.A.1.2.2, SS.A.1.2.3, SS.A.2.2.1, SS.A.2.2.6, SS.A.3.2.1, SS.A.3.2.4, SS.B.1.2.1.(5.1), SS.B.1.2.4, SS.B.2.2.3.(5.1), SS.B.2.2.4, SS.D.1.2.2.(5.1)**		Making Social Studies Relevant Video Unit 2 Visual Summary Poster Game Time! Assessment Program Unit 2 Test, Standard Test, pp. 39–43 Performance Tasks, pp. 44–45 ▶ THE AMAZING WRITING MACHINE ▶ TIMELINER ▶ INTERNET	

Planning Chart

	FLORIDA GRADE LEVEL EXPECTATIONS	FCAT WRITES	RESOURCES INCLUDING	FCAT PRACTICE
UNIT INTRODUCTION Introduce the Unit Preview Set the Scene with Literature **Going to the Colonies** Printed at London for Fylke Clifton in 1630 pp. 166–171	**SS.A.4.2.2.(5.1)** Knows significant events in the colonization of North America, including but not limited to the Jamestown and Plymouth settlements, and the formation of the thirteen original colonies. **SS.A.4.2.2.(5.2)** Understands selected aspects of everyday life in Colonial America (for example, impact of religions, types of work, use of land, leisure activities, relations with Native Americans, slavery). **SS.B.1.2.1.(5.1)** Extends and refines use of maps, globes, charts, graphs, and other geographic tools including map keys and symbols to gather and interpret data and to draw conclusions about physical patterns (for example, in the United States). **SS.A.1.2.1.(5.1), SS.A.1.2.2, SS.A.1.2.3, SS.A.3.2.3, SS.A.3.2.4, SS.B.1.2.2.(5.1), SS.B.2.2.2.(5.1), SS.B.2.2.3.(5.1), SS.B.2.2.4, SS.D.1.2.2.(5.1)**		▶ **TECHNOLOGY** Unit 3 Visual Summary Poster Unit 3 Home Letter Unit 3 Text on Tape Audiocassette Video Experiences: Social Studies ▶ **TimeLiner**	
CHAPTER 5				
LESSON 1 **The Spanish Borderlands** pp. 173–177 *(continued)*	**SS.A.4.2.2.(5.1)** Knows significant events in the colonization of North America, including but not limited to the Jamestown and Plymouth settlements, and the formation of the thirteen original colonies. **SS.A.4.2.2.(5.2)** Understands selected aspects of everyday life in Colonial America (for example, impact of religions, types of work, use of land, leisure activities, relations with Native Americans, slavery). **SS.B.2.2.2.(5.1)** Understands ways the physical environment supports and constrains human activities in the United States. **SS.D.2.2.1.(5.1)** Understands economic specialization and how specialization generally affects costs, amount of goods and services produced, and interdependence. **SS.A.1.2.1.(5.1), SS.A.1.2.2, SS.A.1.2.3, SS.A.3.2.4., SS.A.4.2.1.(5.1),**	**Narrative Writing – Business Letter** Two of Spain's main goals in settling the North American borderlands were to expand its economy and to bring the Catholic faith to the Indians. Imagine that you are a Franciscan monk in charge of a mission in southern California. Write a letter to the Spanish king telling him what you are doing to accomplish both of these goals.	Activity Book, p. 29 ▶ **THE AMAZING WRITING MACHINE**	FCAT Practice Book, p. 18

TIME MANAGEMENT

DAY 1	DAY 2	DAY 3	DAY 4	DAY 5	DAY 6	DAY 7
Unit Introduction	Lesson 1	Lesson 2	Lesson 3	Skill	Chapter Review	Chapter Test

	FLORIDA GRADE LEVEL EXPECTATIONS	FCAT WRITES	RESOURCES INCLUDING ▶ TECHNOLOGY	FCAT PRACTICE
(continued) **LESSON 1** The Spanish Borderlands pp. 173–177	SS.A.4.2.1.(5.2), SS.A.6.2.2, SS.A.6.2.3, SS.B.1.2.1.(5.1), SS.B.1.2.2.(5.1), SS.B.2.2.3.(5.1), SS.D.1.2.2.(5.1)			
LESSON 2 Growth of New France pp. 178–182	**SS.A.3.2.3** The student understands the types of laws and government systems that have developed since the Renaissance (e.g., the development of democracy, the rise of totalitarian governments and dictatorships, communism and absolutism). **SS.A.4.2.1.(5.1)** Knows selected European explorers and the territories they explored in North America. **SS.A.4.2.1.(5.2)** Understands selected geographic, economic, political, and cultural factors that characterized early exploration of the Americas (for example, impact on Native Americans, war between colonial powers, the institution of slavery). **SS.B.1.2.2.(5.1)** Knows how regions in the United States are constructed according to physical criteria and human criteria. SS.A.1.2.1.(5.1), SS.A.1.2.2, SS.A.1.2.3, SS.A.3.2.4, SS.A.4.2.2.(5.1), SS.A.4.2.2.(5.2), SS.B.1..2.1(5.1), SS.B.1.2.4, SS.B.2.2.2.(5.1), SS.B.2.2.3.(5.1), SS.D.2.2.1.(5.1)	**Expository Writing – Compare and Contrast** Write a paragraph explaining the difference between a royal colony and a proprietary colony. Which would you rather have lived in? Why? Share your paragraph with your classmates.	Activity Book, p. 30	FCAT Practice Book, p. 19
LESSON 3 Thirteen British Colonies pp. 183–190 *(continued)*	**SS.A.4.2.2.(5.1)** Knows significant events in the colonization of North America, including but not limited to the Jamestown and Plymouth settlements, and the formation of the thirteen original colonies. **SS.A.4.2.2.(5.2)** Understands selected aspects of everyday life in Colonial America (for example, impact of religions, types of work, use of land, leisure activities, relations with Native Americans, slavery). **SS.B.1.2.2.(5.1)** Knows how regions in the United States are constructed according to physical criteria and human criteria. **SS.B.2.2.2.(5.1)** Understands ways the physical environment supports and constrains human activities in the United States.	**Persuasive Writing – Opinion** Imagine that you are an English citizen who is being treated unfairly because of your religion. You feel that the only way to gain religious freedom for yourself and your family is to leave England and go to the American colonies. Your cousin has settled in the Massachusetts Bay colony and has written letters urging you to join him there. You, however, feel that Maryland would be the best place to settle. Write a letter to your	Activity Book, p. 31 ▶ **THE AMAZING WRITING MACHINE**	FCAT Practice Book, p. 20

Planning Chart

	FLORIDA GRADE LEVEL EXPECTATIONS	FCAT WRITES	RESOURCES INCLUDING ► TECHNOLOGY	FCAT PRACTICE
(continued) **LESSON 3** Thirteen British Colonies pp. 183–190	SS.A.1.2.1.(5.1), SS.A.1.2.2, SS.A.1.2.3, SS.A.3.2.3, SS.A.4.2.1.(5.1), SS.A.4.2.1.(5.2), SS.A.4.2.4.(5.1), SS.A.4.2.4.(5.2), SS.B.1.2.1.(5.1), SS.B.2.2.3.(5.1), SS.D.2.2.1.(5.1)	cousin, explaining your decision and persuading him to join you in Maryland.		
SKILL Classify Information p. 191	**SS.A.1.2.2** Uses a variety of methods and sources to understand history (e.g., interpreting diaries, letters, newspapers; and reading maps and graphs) and knows the difference between primary and secondary sources. **SS.A.1.2.3** Understands broad categories of time in years, decades, and centuries. **SS.B.1.2.1.(5.1)** Extends and refines use of maps, globes, charts, graphs, and other geographic tools including map keys and symbols to gather and interpret data and to draw conclusions about physical patterns (for example, in the United States). **SS.B.1.2.2.(5.1)** Knows how regions in the United States are constructed according to physical criteria and human criteria. **SS.A.4.2.2.(5.1)**		Activity Book, p. 32 Transparency 14	
CHAPTER REVIEW pp. 192–193	**SS.A.4.2.1.(5.1)** Knows selected European explorers and the territories they explored in North America. **SS.A.4.2.2.(5.1)** Knows significant events in the colonization of North America, including but not limited to the Jamestown and Plymouth settlements, and the formation of the thirteen original colonies. **SS.A.4.2.2.(5.2)** Understands selected aspects of everyday life in Colonial America (for example, impact of religions, types of work, use of land, leisure activities, relations with Native Americans, slavery). **SS.B.1.2.2.(5.1)** Knows how regions in the United States are constructed according to physical criteria and human criteria. SS.A.1.2.1.(5.1), SS.A.1.2.2, SS.A.1.2.3, SS.A.3.2.3, SS.A.4.2.1.(5.2), SS.A.4.2.4.(5.1), SS.A.4.2.4.(5.2), SS.B.1.2.1.(5.1), SS.B.2.2.2.(5.1), SS.B.2.2.3.(5.1), SS.D.2.2.1.(5.1)		Activity Book, p. 33 Transparency 15 Assessment Program Chapter 5 Test, pp. 47–50 ► THE AMAZING WRITING MACHINE ► TIMELINER ► INTERNET	

Teacher's Notes

Planning Chart

	FLORIDA GRADE LEVEL EXPECTATIONS	FCAT WRITES	RESOURCES INCLUDING ▶ TECHNOLOGY	FCAT PRACTICE
LESSON 1 Life in Towns and Cities pp. 195–198	**SS.A.4.2.2.(5.2)** Understands selected aspects of everyday life in Colonial America (for example, impact of religions, types of work, use of land, leisure activities, relations with Native Americans, slavery). **SS.B.1.2.2.(5.1)** Knows how regions in the United States are constructed according to physical criteria and human criteria. **SS.B.2.2.1.(5.1)** Understands reasons certain areas of the United States are more densely populated than others. **SS.B.2.2.2.(5.1)** Understands ways the physical environment supports and constrains human activities in the United States. **SS.A.1.2.2, SS.A.1.2.3, SS.A.3.2.3, SS.A.3.2.4, SS.B.1.2.1.(5.1), SS.B.1.2.4, SS.B.2.2.3.(5.1), SS.B.2.2.4, SS.C.1.2.5.(5.1), SS.C.2.2.1.(5.1)**	**Narrative Writing – Personal Experience** Imagine that you are a colonist living in a market town. It is market day, and you must shop for the items your family will need in the coming weeks. You also have many other errands to run while you are in town. Write a paragraph about your market day. Include descriptions of the places you visit, the people you see, and the things you do.	Activity Book, p. 34 ▶ **DECISIONS, DECISIONS**	FCAT Practice Book, p. 21
SKILL Read a Circle Graph p. 199	**SS.A.1.2.2** Uses a variety of methods and sources to understand history (e.g., interpreting diaries, letters, newspapers; and reading maps and graphs) and knows the difference between primary and secondary sources. **SS.A.4.2.2.(5.2)** Understands selected aspects of everyday life in Colonial America (for example, impact of religions, types of work, use of land, leisure activities, relations with Native Americans, slavery). **SS.A.1.2.3, SS.A.3.2.4**		Activity Book, p. 35 Transparency 16	
LESSON 2 Life on Plantations pp. 200–203 *(continued)*	**SS.A.4.2.2.(5.2)** Understands selected aspects of everyday life in Colonial America (for example, impact of religions, types of work, use of land, leisure activities, relations with Native Americans, slavery). **SS.B.2.2.2.(5.1)** Understands ways the physical environment supports and constrains human activities in the United States.	**Persuasive Writing – Letter to the Editor** Imagine that you own a Southern plantation. The African workers on your plantation do not know how to read or write. You believe that all people should be given	Activity Book, p. 36	FCAT Practice Book, p. 22

TIME MANAGEMENT

DAY 1	DAY 2	DAY 3	DAY 4	DAY 5	DAY 6	DAY 7	DAY 8
Lesson 1	Skill	Lesson 2	Lesson 3	Skill	Chapter Review	Chapter Test	Unit Wrap-Up

	FLORIDA GRADE LEVEL EXPECTATIONS	FCAT WRITES	RESOURCES INCLUDING	FCAT PRACTICE
			▶ TECHNOLOGY	
(continued) **LESSON 2** Life on Plantations pp. 200–203	**SS.B.2.2.3.(5.1)** Understands ways human activity has affected the physical environment in various places and times in the United States. **SS.D.2.2.1.(5.1)** Understands economic specialization and how specialization generally affects costs, amount of goods and services produced, and interdependence. **SS.A.1.2.1.(5.1), SS.A.1.2.2, SS.A.1.2.3, SS.A.3.2.3, SS.A.3.2.4, SS.B.1.2.2.(5.1), SS.B.2.2.1.(5.1), SS.B.2.2.4, SS.D.1.2.1.(5.1)**	the opportunity to learn these skills. Write a letter to the editor of a newspaper to convince readers to agree with your point of view.		
LESSON 3 Life on the Frontier pp. 204–207	**SS.A.4.2.2.(5.2)** Understands selected aspects of everyday life in Colonial America (for example, impact of religions, types of work, use of land, leisure activities, relations with Native Americans, slavery). **SS.B.1.2.2.(5.1)** Knows how regions in the United States are constructed according to physical criteria and human criteria. **SS.D.1.2.1.(5.1)** Knows examples from United Sates history that demonstrate an understanding that all decisions involve opportunity costs and that making effective decisions involves considering the costs and the benefits associated with alternative choices. **SS.D.1.2.2.(5.1)** Understands that scarcity of resources requires choices on many levels, from the individual to societal. **SS.A.1.2.1.(5.1), SS.A.1.2.2, SS.A.1.2.3, SS.A.3.2.4, SS.A.4.2.1.(5.2), SS.B.1.2.1.(5.1), SS.B.1.2.4, SS.B.2.2.1.(5.1), SS.B.2.2.2.(5.1), SS.B.2.2.3.(5.1), SS.B.2.2.4**	**Expository Writing – Compare and Contrast** Frontier families made almost everything they needed, including clothing, food, and shelter. Think about eating your favorite food or wearing your favorite outfit. Then write an outline comparing the steps it takes for you to do one of these things with the steps it would take for a frontier girl or boy to do the same.	Activity Book, p. 37 Music Audiocassette ▶ MAPSKILLS	FCAT Practice Book, p. 23
SKILL Use a Product Map pp. 208–209	**SS.A.1.2.2** Uses a variety of methods and sources to understand history (e.g., interpreting diaries, letters, newspapers; and reading maps and graphs) and knows the difference between primary and secondary sources. **SS.B.1.2.1.(5.1)** Extends and refines use of maps, globes, charts, graphs, and other geographic tools including map keys and symbols to gather and interpret data and to draw conclusions about physical patterns (for example, in the United States).		Activity Book, p. 38 Transparency 17 ▶ MAPSKILLS	
(continued)				

Planning Chart

	FLORIDA GRADE LEVEL EXPECTATIONS	FCAT WRITES	RESOURCES INCLUDING ► TECHNOLOGY	FCAT PRACTICE
(continued) **SKILL** **Use a Product Map** pp. 208–209	**SS.B.2.2.2.(5.1)** Understands ways the physical environment supports and constrains human activities in the United States. **SS.B.2.2.3.(5.1)** Understands ways human activity has affected the physical environment in various places and times in the United States. **SS.B.1.2.2.(5.1)**			
CHAPTER REVIEW pp. 210–211	**SS.A.4.2.2.(5.2)** Understands selected aspects of everyday life in Colonial America (for example, impact of religions, types of work, use of land, leisure activities, relations with Native Americans, slavery). **SS.B.1.2.1.(5.1)** Extends and refines use of maps, globes, charts, graphs, and other geographic tools including map keys and symbols to gather and interpret data and to draw conclusions about physical patterns (for example, in the United States). **SS.B.1.2.2.(5.1)** Knows how regions in the United States are constructed according to physical criteria and human criteria. **SS.B.2.2.2.(5.1)** Understands ways the physical environment supports and constrains human activities in the United States. **SS.A.1.2.1.(5.1), SS.A.1.2.2, SS.A.3.2.3, SS.A.3.2.4, SS.A.4.2.1.(5.2), SS.B.1.2.4, SS.B.2.2.1.(5.1), SS.B.2.2.3.(5.1), SS.B.2.2.4, SS.D.1.2.1.(5.1), SS.D.2.2.1.(5.1)**		Activity Book, p. 39 Transparency 18 Assessment Program Chapter 6 Test, pp. 51–54 ► THE AMAZING WRITING MACHINE ► INTERNET	
UNIT WRAP-UP Making Social Studies Relevant Visual Summary Unit 3 Review pp. 212–217	**SS.A.4.2.2.(5.1)** Knows significant events in the colonization of North America, including but not limited to the Jamestown and Plymouth settlements, and the formation of the thirteen original colonies. **SS.A.4.2.2.(5.2)** Understands selected aspects of everyday life in Colonial America (for example, impact of religions, types of work, use of land, leisure activities, relations with Native Americans, slavery). **SS.B.1.2.1.(5.1)** Extends and refines use of maps, globes, charts, graphs, and other geographic tools including map keys and symbols to gather and interpret data and to draw conclusions about physical patterns (for example, in the United States).		Making Social Studies Relevant Video Unit 3 Visual Summary Poster Game Time! Assessment Program Unit 3 Test, Standard Test, pp. 55–59 Performance Tasks, pp. 60–61 ► THE AMAZING WRITING MACHINE ► TIMELINER ► INTERNET	

(continued)

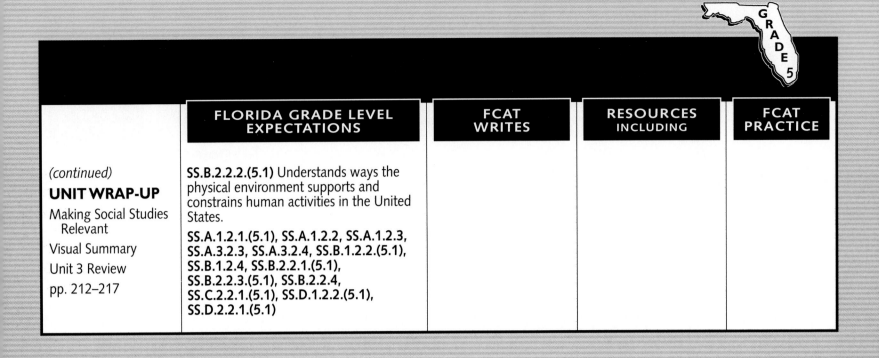

	FLORIDA GRADE LEVEL EXPECTATIONS	FCAT WRITES	RESOURCES INCLUDING	FCAT PRACTICE
(continued) **UNIT WRAP-UP** Making Social Studies Relevant Visual Summary Unit 3 Review pp. 212–217	**SS.B.2.2.2.(5.1)** Understands ways the physical environment supports and constrains human activities in the United States. **SS.A.1.2.1.(5.1), SS.A.1.2.2, SS.A.1.2.3, SS.A.3.2.3, SS.A.3.2.4, SS.B.1.2.2.(5.1), SS.B.1.2.4, SS.B.2.2.1.(5.1), SS.B.2.2.3.(5.1), SS.B.2.2.4, SS.C.2.2.1.(5.1), SS.D.1.2.2.(5.1), SS.D.2.2.1.(5.1)**			

Teacher's Notes

_____

_____

_____

_____

_____

_____

_____

_____

_____

_____

Planning Chart

	FLORIDA GRADE LEVEL EXPECTATIONS	FCAT WRITES	RESOURCES INCLUDING	FCAT PRACTICE
UNIT INTRODUCTION Introduce the Unit Preview Set the Scene with Literature **Guns for General Washington** by Seymour Reit pp. 218–223	**SS.A.4.2.3.(5.1)** Understands reasons Americans and those who led them went to war to win independence from England. **SS.A.4.2.3.(5.2)** Knows significant events between 1756 and 1776 that led to the outbreak of the American Revolution (for example, the French and Indian War, the Stamp Act, the Boston Tea Party). **SS.A.4.2.3.(5.3)** Knows selected aspects of the major military campaigns of the Revolutionary War. **SS.B.1.2.1.(5.1)** Extends and refines use of maps, globes, charts, graphs, and other geographic tools including map keys and symbols to gather and interpret data and to draw conclusions about physical patterns (for example, in the United States). **SS.A.1.2.1.(5.1), SS.A.1.2.2, SS.A.1.2.3, SS.A.3.2.3, SS.A.4.2.2.(5.2), SS.A.4.2.4.(5.1), SS.A.4.2.4.(5.2), SS.B.1.2.2.(5.1), SS.B.2.2.1.(5.1), SS.B.2.2.2.(5.1), SS.C.2.2.1.(5.1), SS.C.2.2.2.(5.1), SS.C.2.2.5.(5.1), SS.D.1.2.1.(5.1), SS.D.1.2.2.(5.1)**		▶ **TECHNOLOGY** Unit 4 Visual Summary Poster Unit 4 Home Letter Unit 4 Text on Tape Audiocassette Video Experiences: Social Studies ▶ **TIMELINER**	

CHAPTER 7

	FLORIDA GRADE LEVEL EXPECTATIONS	FCAT WRITES	RESOURCES INCLUDING	FCAT PRACTICE
LESSON 1 Government in the Colonies pp. 225–228 *(continued)*	**SS.A.3.2.3** The student understands the types of laws and government systems that have developed since the Renaissance (e.g., the development of democracy, the rise of totalitarian governments and dictatorships, communism and absolutism). **SS.A.4.2.3.(5.1)** Understands reasons Americans and those who led them went to war to win independence from England. **SS.A.4.2.3.(5.2)** Knows significant events between 1756 and 1776 that led to the outbreak of the American Revolution (for example, the French and Indian War, the Stamp Act, the Boston Tea Party).	**Expository Writing – Observation** Historical maps give information about places as they were in the past. Compare the map of North America on page 226 with the map of North America on page 229. What changes do you see from 1750 to 1763 in the lands claimed by France and those claimed by England? Write one or two paragraphs about your observations.	Activity Book, p. 40	FCAT Practice Book, p. 24

TIME MANAGEMENT

DAY 1	DAY 2	DAY 3	DAY 4	DAY 5	DAY 6	DAY 7	DAY 8	DAY 9
Unit Introduction	Lesson 1	Skill	Counterpoints	Lesson 2	Lesson 3	Skill	Chapter Review	Chapter Test

	FLORIDA GRADE LEVEL EXPECTATIONS	FCAT WRITES	RESOURCES INCLUDING ▶ TECHNOLOGY	FCAT PRACTICE
(continued) **LESSON 1** Government in the Colonies pp. 225–228	**SS.C.2.2.5.(5.1)** Knows what constitutes personal, political, and economic rights and why they are important (for example, right to vote, assemble, lobby, own property and business). **SS.A.1.2.1.(5.1), SS.A.1.2.2, SS.A.1.2.3, SS.A.4.2.2.(5.2), SS.B.1.2.1.(5.1), SS.B.1.2.2.(5.1), SS.C.2.2.1.(5.1), SS.C.2.2.2.(5.1), SS.C.2.2.3.(5.1), SS.C.2.2.4.(5.1), SS.D.1.2.1.(5.1), SS.D.2.2.4.(5.1)**			
SKILL Use a Historical Map p. 229	**SS.A.3.2.3** The student understands the types of laws and government systems that have developed since the Renaissance (e.g., the development of democracy, the rise of totalitarian governments and dictatorships, communism and absolutism). **SS.B.1.2.1.(5.1)** Extends and refines use of maps, globes, charts, graphs, and other geographic tools including map keys and symbols to gather and interpret data and to draw conclusions about physical patterns (for example, in the United States). **SS.B.1.2.2.(5.1)** Knows how regions in the United States are constructed according to physical criteria and human criteria. **SS.A.1.2.2, SS.A.1.2.3**		Activity Book, p. 41 Transparency 19 ▶ MAPSKILLS	
COUNTERPOINTS Self-Government or British Rule? pp. 230–231	**SS.A.4.2.3.(5.1)** Understands reasons Americans and those who led them went to war to win independence from England. **SS.A.4.2.3.(5.2)** Knows significant events between 1756 and 1776 that led to the outbreak of the American Revolution (for example, the French and Indian War, the Stamp Act, the Boston Tea Party). **SS.C.2.2.5.(5.1)** Knows what constitutes personal, political, and economic rights and why they are important (for example, right to vote, assemble, lobby, own property and business). **SS.D.2.2.4.(5.1)** Knows ways the Federal government provides goods and services through taxation and borrowing. **SS.A.1.2.2, SS.A.3.2.3, SS.A.4.2.2.(5.2)**		▶ THE AMAZING WRITING MACHINE	

Planning Chart

	FLORIDA GRADE LEVEL EXPECTATIONS	FCAT WRITES	RESOURCES INCLUDING	FCAT PRACTICE
LESSON 2 **Quarrels and Conflicts** pp. 232–237	**SS.A.4.2.3.(5.1)** Understands reasons Americans and those who led them went to war to win independence from England. **SS.A.4.2.3.(5.2)** Knows significant events between 1756 and 1776 that led to the outbreak of the American Revolution (for example, the French and Indian War, the Stamp Act, the Boston Tea Party). **SS.C.2.2.5.(5.1)** Knows what constitutes personal, political, and economic rights and why they are important (for example, right to vote, assemble, lobby, own property and business). **SS.D.1.2.1.(5.1)** Knows examples from United Sates history that demonstrate an understanding that all decisions involve opportunity costs and that making effective decisions involves considering the costs and the benefits associated with alternative choices. **SS.A.1.2.1.(5.1), SS.A.1.2.2, SS.A.1.2.3, SS.C.2.2.1.(5.1), SS.C.2.2.2.(5.1), SS.C.2.2.3.(5.1), SS.D.1.2.2.(5.1), SS.D.2.2.1.(5.1), SS.D.2.2.4.(5.1)**	**Persuasive Writing – Request** You are an American colonist opposed to the Stamp Act. Write a petition to King George III, requesting that the tax be repealed. State your reasons, being sure to include examples of the problems the Stamp Act has caused in the colonies.	▶ **TECHNOLOGY** Activity Book, p. 42 Music Audiocassette	FCAT Practice Book, p. 25
LESSON 3 **Colonists Unite** pp. 238–242	**SS.A.1.2.1.(5.1)** Extends and refines understanding of the effects of individuals, ideas, and decisions on historical events (for example, in the United States). **SS.A.4.2.3.(5.1)** Understands reasons Americans and those who led them went to war to win independence from England. **SS.A.4.2.3.(5.2)** Knows significant events between 1756 and 1776 that led to the outbreak of the American Revolution (for example, the French and Indian War, the Stamp Act, the Boston Tea Party). **SS.A.4.2.3.(5.3)** Knows selected aspects of the major military campaigns of the Revolutionary War. **SS.A.1.2.2, SS.A.1.2.3, SS.B.1.2.1.(5.1), SS.C.2.2.1.(5.1), SS.C.2.2.2.(5.1), SS.C.2.2.3.(5.1), SS.C.2.2.5.(5.1), SS.D.1.2.1.(5.1), SS.D.1.2.2.(5.1), SS.D.2.2.4.(5.1)**	**Narrative Writing – Personal Experience** Imagine that you are a member of the Sons of Liberty. Write a paragraph describing your feelings and experiences during the Boston Tea Party.	Activity Book, p. 43	FCAT Practice Book, p. 26
SKILL **Make Economic Choices** p. 243 *(continued)*	**SS.A.4.2.3.(5.2)** Knows significant events between 1756 and 1776 that led to the outbreak of the American Revolution (for example, the French and Indian War, the Stamp Act, the Boston Tea Party).		Activity Book, p. 44 Transparency 20 ▶ **LOOKING AHEAD:** EARNING, SPENDING, SAVING	

	FLORIDA GRADE LEVEL EXPECTATIONS	FCAT WRITES	RESOURCES INCLUDING ▶ TECHNOLOGY	FCAT PRACTICE
(continued) **SKILL** **Make Economic Choices** p. 243	**SS.D.1.2.1.(5.1)** Knows examples from United Sates history that demonstrate an understanding that all decisions involve opportunity costs and that making effective decisions involves considering the costs and the benefits associated with alternative choices. **SS.D.1.2.2.(5.1)** Understands that scarcity of resources requires choices on many levels, from the individual to societal. **SS.D.2.2.4.(5.1)** Knows ways the Federal government provides goods and services through taxation and borrowing (for example, highways, military defense). **SS.A.1.2.3, SS.A.3.2.3, SS.A.4.2.3.(5.1)**			
CHAPTER REVIEW pp.244–245	**SS.A.4.2.3.(5.1)** Understands reasons Americans and those who led them went to war to win independence from England. **SS.A.4.2.3.(5.2)** Knows significant events between 1756 and 1776 that led to the outbreak of the American Revolution (for example, the French and Indian War, the Stamp Act, the Boston Tea Party). **SS.B.1.2.1.(5.1)** Extends and refines use of maps, globes, charts, graphs, and other geographic tools including map keys and symbols to gather and interpret data and to draw conclusions about physical patterns (for example, in the United States). **SS.D.1.2.1.(5.1)** Knows examples from United Sates history that demonstrate an understanding that all decisions involve opportunity costs and that making effective decisions involves considering the costs and the benefits associated with alternative choices. **SS.A.1.2.2, SS.A.1.2.3, SS.A.3.2.3, SS.A.4.2.3.(5.3), SS.C.2.2.1.(5.1), SS.C.2.2.2.(5.1), SS.C.2.2.3.(5.1), SS.C.2.2.4.(5.1), SS.C.2.2.5.(5.1), SS.D.2.2.4.(5.1)**		Activity Book, p. 45 Transparency 21 Assessment Program Chapter 7 Test, pp. 63–66 ▶ THE AMAZING WRITING MACHINE ▶ TIMELINER ▶ INTERNET	

Planning Chart

	FLORIDA GRADE LEVEL EXPECTATIONS	FCAT WRITES	RESOURCES INCLUDING ▶ TECHNOLOGY	FCAT PRACTICE
LESSON 1 **At War with the Homeland** pp. 247–250	SS.A.4.2.3.(5.2) Knows significant events between 1756 and 1776 that led to the outbreak of the American Revolution (for example, the French and Indian War, the Stamp Act, the Boston Tea Party). SS.A.4.2.3.(5.3) Knows selected aspects of the major military campaigns of the Revolutionary War. SS.A.4.2.4.(5.1) Knows the history of events and the historic figures responsible for historical documents important to the founding of the United States (for example, the Declaration of Independence, the United States Constitution, the Bill of Rights). SS.A.4.2.4.(5.2) Knows selected principal ideas expressed in significant historical documents important to the founding of the United States (including but not limited to the Declaration of Independence, the United States Constitution, the Bill of Rights, the Federalist Papers). SS.A.1.2.1.(5.1), SS.A.1.2.2, SS.A.1.2.3, SS.A.4.2.3.(5.1), SS.A.4.2.3.(5.4), SS.B.1.2.1.(5.1), SS.C.2.2.1.(5.1), SS.C.2.2.2.(5.1), SS.C.2.2.5.(5.1), SS.D.1.2.1.(5.1), SS.D.1.2.2.(5.1)	**Expository Writing – Compare and Contrast** Think about the many differences between the Continental and British forces at the beginning of the American Revolution. Then write a paragraph comparing the battle strategies of the two armies. Give your opinion about which strategy would be the most effective.	Activity Book, p. 46 ▶ THE AMAZING WRITING MACHINE	FCAT Practice Book, p. 27
SKILL **Read a Political Cartoon** p. 251	SS.A.1.2.2 Uses a variety of methods and sources to understand history (e.g., interpreting diaries, letters, newspapers; and reading maps and graphs) and knows the difference between primary and secondary sources. SS.A.4.2.4.(5.1) Knows the history of events and the historic figures responsible for historical documents important to the founding of the United States (for example, the Declaration of Independence, the United States Constitution, the Bill of Rights).		Activity Book, p. 47 Transparency 22	

(continued)

TIME MANAGEMENT								
DAY 1	**DAY 2**	**DAY 3**	**DAY 4**	**DAY 5**	**DAY 6**	**DAY 7**	**DAY 8**	**DAY 9**
Lesson 1	Skill	Lesson 2	Lesson 3	Lesson 4	Lesson 5	Chapter Review	Chapter Test	Unit Wrap-Up

	FLORIDA GRADE LEVEL EXPECTATIONS	FCAT WRITES	RESOURCES INCLUDING ► TECHNOLOGY	FCAT PRACTICE
(continued) **SKILL** **Read a Political Cartoon** p. 251	**SS.A.4.2.4.(5.2)** Knows selected principal ideas expressed in significant historical documents important to the founding of the United States (including but not limited to the Declaration of Independence, the United States Constitution, the Bill of Rights, the Federalist Papers). **SS.B.1.2.2.(5.1)** Knows how regions in the United States are constructed according to physical criteria and human criteria. **SS.A.1.2.3, SS.A.3.2.1, SS.B.1.2.4**			
LESSON 2 **The Decision for Independence** pp. 252–255	**SS.A.4.2.3.(5.1)** Understands reasons Americans and those who led them went to war to win independence from England. **SS.A.4.2.3.(5.2)** Knows significant events between 1756 and 1776 that led to the outbreak of the American Revolution (for example, the French and Indian War, the Stamp Act, the Boston Tea Party). **SS.A.4.2.4.(5.1)** Knows the history of events and the historic figures responsible for historical documents important to the founding of the United States (for example, the Declaration of Independence, the United States Constitution, the Bill of Rights). **SS.A.4.2.4.(5.2)** Knows selected principal ideas expressed in significant historical documents important to the founding of the United States (including but not limited to the Declaration of Independence, the United States Constitution, the Bill of Rights, the Federalist Papers). **SS.A.1.2.1.(5.1), SS.A.1.2.2, SS.A.1.2.3, SS.A.3.2.3, SS.B.1.2.2.(5.1), SS.C.2.2.5.(5.1)**	**Narrative Writing – Journal** John Adams said that Independence Day should be remembered "...with pomp and parade, with shows, games, sports, guns, bells, bonfires, and illuminations." Think about whether or not his wish is still being carried out today. Then write a paragraph describing how you celebrated last Independence Day.	Activity Book, p. 48	FCAT Practice Book, p. 28
LESSON 3 **Americans Take Sides** pp. 256–259	**SS.A.4.2.3.(5.1)** Understands reasons Americans and those who led them went to war to win independence from England. **SS.B.1.2.2.(5.1)** Knows how regions in the United States are constructed according to physical criteria and human criteria. **SS.B.1.2.5.(5.1)** Understands varying perceptions of regions throughout the United States. **SS.A.1.2.2, SS.A.1.2.3, SS.D.1.2.2.(5.1), SS.D.2.2.1.(5.1)**	**Expository Writing – Biography** Mary Ludwig Hays, Phillis Wheatley, Abigail Adams, and Mercy Otis Warren were all women who supported the Patriot cause during the American Revolution. Learn more about one of these women, and write a short biography to share with your class.	Activity Book, p. 49 ► THE AMAZING WRITING MACHINE	FCAT Practice Book, p. 29

Planning Chart

	FLORIDA GRADE LEVEL EXPECTATIONS	FCAT WRITES	RESOURCES INCLUDING	FCAT PRACTICE
LESSON 4 Learn History Through Literature 📖 **Samuel's Choice** by Richard Berleth pp. 260–263	**SS.A.1.2.3** Understands broad categories of time in years, decades, and centuries. **SS.B.2.2.2.(5.1)** Understands ways the physical environment supports and constrains human activities in the United States. **SS.C.2.2.1.(5.1)** Understands the importance of participation through community service, civic improvement, and political activities. **SS.A.1.2.2., SS.C.2.2.2.(5.1)**	**Narrative Writing – Story** Think about what happened to the main character in the literature selection *Samuel's Choice.* Then write a story about Samuel in the years after the American Revolution.	▶ **TECHNOLOGY** Activity Book, p. 50	FCAT Practice Book, p. 30
LESSON 5 Victory and Independence pp. 264–269	**SS.A.4.2.3.(5.3)** Knows selected aspects of major military campaigns of the Revolutionary War. **SS.A.4.2.3.(5.4)** Knows reasons why the colonies were able to defeat the British. **SS.A.4.2.4.(5.1)** Knows the history of events and the historic figures responsible for historical documents important to the founding of the United States (for example, the Declaration of Independence, the United States Constitution, the Bill of Rights). **SS.A.4.2.4.(5.2)** Knows selected principal ideas expressed in significant historical documents important to the founding of the United States (including but not limited to the Declaration of Independence, the United States Constitution, the Bill of Rights, the Federalist Papers). **SS.A.1.2.1.(5.1), SS.A.1.2.2, SS.A.1.2.3, SS.A.3.2.3, SS.A.4.2.3.(5.1), SS.B.1.2.1.(5.1), SS.B.1.2.2.(5.1), SS.B.2.2.2.(5.1), SS.D.1.2.1.(5.1), SS.D.1.2.2.(5.1)**	**Persuasive Writing – Opinion** The American Revolution was a challenging time for everyone involved. Imagine that you are a newspaper reporter. Then consider what you have learned about the differences between the Continental and British armies. Write an article intended to persuade readers that the Patriots could not have won the American Revolution without help from other countries.	Activity Book, p. 51 ▶ **DECISIONS, DECISIONS** ▶ **THE AMAZING WRITING MACHINE**	FCAT Practice Book, p. 31
CHAPTER REVIEW pp. 270–271	**SS.A.4.2.3.(5.1)** Understands reasons Americans and those who led them went to war to win independence from England. **SS.A.4.2.3.(5.2)** Knows significant events between 1756 and 1776 that led to the outbreak of the American Revolution (for example, the French and Indian War, the Stamp Act, the Boston Tea Party). **SS.A.4.2.3.(5.3)** Knows selected aspects of major military campaigns of the Revolutionary War. **SS.A.4.2.3.(5.4)** Knows reasons why the colonies were able to defeat the British. *(continued)*		Activity Book, p. 52 Transparency 23 Assessment Program Chapter 8 Test, pp. 67–70 ▶ **THE AMAZING WRITING MACHINE** ▶ **TIMELINER** ▶ **INTERNET**	

	FLORIDA GRADE LEVEL EXPECTATIONS	FCAT WRITES	RESOURCES INCLUDING	FCAT PRACTICE
(continued) **CHAPTER REVIEW** pp. 270–271	SS.A.1.2.3, SS.A.3.2.3, SS.A.4.2.4.(5.1), SS.A.4.2.4.(5.2), SS.B.1.2.2.(5.1), SS.B.2.2.2.(5.1), SS.D.1.2.1.(5.1)			
UNIT WRAP-UP *Making Social Studies Relevant* Visual Summary Unit 4 Review pp. 272–277	**SS.A.1.2.3.(5.1)** Constructs and labels a time line based on a historical reading (for example, about United States history). **SS.A.4.2.3.(5.1)** Understands reasons Americans and those who led them went to war to win independence from England. **SS.A.4.2.3.(5.2)** Knows significant events between 1756 and 1776 that led to the outbreak of the American Revolution (for example, the French and Indian War, the Stamp Act, the Boston Tea Party). **SS.B.1.2.1.(5.1)** Extends and refines use of maps, globes, charts, graphs, and other geographic tools including map keys and symbols to gather and interpret data and to draw conclusions about physical patterns (for example, in the United States). SS.A.1.2.1.(5.1), SS.A.1.2.2, SS.A.1.2.3, SS.A.3.2.3, SS.A.4.2.3.(5.3), SS.A.4.2.3.(5.4), SS.A.4.2.4.(5.1), SS.A.4.2.4.(5.2), SS.B.1.2.1.(5.1), SS.B.1.2.2.(5.1), SS.C.2.2.1.(5.1), SS.C.2.2.5.(5.1), SS.C.2.2.5.(5.2), SS.D.1.2.1.(5.1), SS.D.2.2.4.(5.1)		*Making Social Studies Relevant* Video Unit 4 Visual Summary Poster Game Time! Assessment Program Unit 4 Test, Standard Test, pp. 71–75 Performance Tasks, pp. 76–77 ▶ THE AMAZING WRITING MACHINE ▶ TIMELINER ▶ INTERNET	

Teacher's Notes

_____

_____

_____

_____

Planning Chart

	FLORIDA GRADE LEVEL EXPECTATIONS	FCAT WRITES	RESOURCES INCLUDING	FCAT PRACTICE
UNIT INTRODUCTION Introduce the Unit Preview Set the Scene with Literature 📖 **Shh! We're Writing the Constitution** by Jean Fritz pp. 278–283	**SS.A.1.2.1.(5.1)** Extends and refines understanding of the effects of individuals, ideas, and decisions on historical events (for example, in the United States). **SS.A.4.2.4.(5.1)** Knows the history of events and the historic figures responsible for historical documents important to the founding of the United States (for example, the Declaration of Independence, the United States Constitution, the Bill of Rights). **SS.B.1.2.1.(5.1)** Extends and refines use of maps, globes, charts, graphs, and other geographic tools including map keys and symbols to gather and interpret data and to draw conclusions about physical patterns (for example, in the United States). **SS.B.1.2.2.(5.1)** Knows how regions in the United States are constructed according to physical criteria and human criteria. **SS.A.1.2.2, SS.A.1.2.3, SS.A.3.2.2., SS.A.3.2.3, SS.B.1.2.5.(5.1), SS.B.2.2.1.(5.1), SS.C.1.2.1.(5.1), SS.C.1.2.1.(5.2), SS.C.1.2.2.(5.1), SS.C.1.2.2.(5.2), SS.C.1.2.5.(5.1). SS.C.2.2.1.(5.1), SS.C.2.2.2.(5.1), SS.C.2.2.3.(5.1), SS.C.2.2.5.(5.1), SS.D.1.2.2.(5.1)**		▶ **TECHNOLOGY** Unit 5 Visual Summary Poster Unit 5 Home Letter Unit 5 Text on Tape Audiocassette Video Experiences: Social Studies ▶ **TIMELINER**	

CHAPTER 9

	FLORIDA GRADE LEVEL EXPECTATIONS	FCAT WRITES	RESOURCES INCLUDING	FCAT PRACTICE
LESSON 1 **The Articles of Confederation** pp. 285–289 *(continued)*	**SS.A.4.2.4.(5.1)** Knows the history of events and the historic figures responsible for historical documents important to the founding of the United States (for example, the Declaration of Independence, the United States Constitution, the Bill of Rights). **SS.A.4.2.4.(5.2)** Knows selected principal ideas expressed in significant historical documents important to the founding of the United States (including but not limited to the Declaration of Independence, the United States Constitution, the Bill of Rights, the Federalist Papers).	**Expository Writing – Outline** In 1781 the states accepted a plan for a new central government that would bring them together under "a firm league of friendship." Think about this new plan, called the Articles of Confederation. Then write an outline for a paper that would explain the main duties of Congress under the new government.	Activity Book, p. 53	FCAT Practice Book, p. 32

TIME MANAGEMENT

DAY 1	DAY 2	DAY 3	DAY 4	DAY 5	DAY 6	DAY 7	DAY 8	DAY 9	DAY 10
Unit Introduction	Lesson 1	Lesson 2	Skill	Lesson 3	Skill	Lesson 4	Lesson 5	Chapter Review	Chapter Test

	FLORIDA GRADE LEVEL EXPECTATIONS	FCAT WRITES	RESOURCES INCLUDING ▶ TECHNOLOGY	FCAT PRACTICE
(continued) **LESSON 1** The Articles of Confederation pp. 285–289	**SS.D.2.2.2.(5.1)** Understands the roles that money plays in a market economy. **SS.A.1.2.1.(5.1), SS.A.1.2.2, SS.A.1.2.3, SS.A.3.2.3, SS.B.1.2.1.(5.1), SS.B.1.2.2.(5.1), SS.C.2.2.1.(5.1), SS.C.2.2.5.(5.1), SS.D.1.2.1.(5.1), SS.D.1.2.2.(5.1), SS.D.1.2.3.(5.1), SS.D.2.2.1.(5.1), SS.D.2.2.3.(5.1), SS.D.2.2.4.(5.1)**			
LESSON 2 A New Plan of Government pp. 290–293	**SS.A.4.2.4.(5.1)** Knows the history of events and the historic figures responsible for historical documents important to the founding of the United States (for example, the Declaration of Independence, the United States Constitution, the Bill of Rights). **SS.A.4.2.4.(5.2)** Knows selected principal ideas expressed in significant historical documents important to the founding of the United States (including but not limited to the Declaration of Independence, the United States Constitution, the Bill of Rights, the Federalist Papers). **SS.C.1.2.1.(5.1)** Understands the functions of government under the framework of the United States constitution. **SS.C.1.2.5.(5.1)** Knows basic things the United States government does in one's school, community, state, and nation. **SS.A.1.2.1.(5.1), S.A.1.2.2, SS.A.1.2.3.(5.1), SS.A.3.2.3, SS.B.1.2.1.(5.1), SS.C.1.2.4.(5.1), SS.C.2.2.1.(5.1), SS.C.2.2.3.(5.1)**	**Persuasive Writing – Business Letter** Imagine that you are a delegate to the Annapolis Convention. You have decided to send a letter to Congress, asking it to call a meeting to discuss the problems with the Articles of Confederation. Write a letter to persuade Congress that this meeting is important. In your letter, be sure to include reasons you believe the Articles of Confederation need to be changed.	Activity Book, p. 54 ▶ THE AMAZING WRITING MACHINE	FCAT Practice Book, p. 33
SKILL Figure Travel Time and Distance pp. 294–295	**SS.A.4.2.4.(5.1)** Knows the history of events and the historic figures responsible for historical documents important to the founding of the United States (for example, the Declaration of Independence, the United States Constitution, the Bill of Rights). **SS.B.1.2.1.(5.1)** Extends and refines use of maps, globes, charts, graphs, and other geographic tools including map keys and symbols to gather and interpret data and to draw conclusions about physical patterns (for example, in the United States). **SS.A.1.2.2, SS.A.1.2.3**		Activity Book, p. 55 Transparency 24 ▶ MAPSKILLS	

Planning Chart

	FLORIDA GRADE LEVEL EXPECTATIONS	FCAT WRITES	RESOURCES INCLUDING	FCAT PRACTICE
LESSON 3 Debates and Compromises pp. 296–300	**SS.A.4.2.4.(5.1)** Knows the history of events and the historic figures responsible for historical documents important to the founding of the United States (for example, the Declaration of Independence, the United States Constitution, the Bill of Rights). **SS.A.4.2.4.(5.2)** Knows selected principal ideas expressed in significant historical documents important to the founding of the United States (including but not limited to the Declaration of Independence, the United States Constitution, the Bill of Rights, the Federalist Papers). **SS.C.1.2.1.(5.1)** Understands the functions of government under the framework of the United States constitution. **SS.C.1.2.1.(5.2)** Understands the branches of federal government and their main roles. **SS.A.1.2.1.(5.1), SS.A.3.2.3, SS.B.1.2.1.(5.1), SS.C.1.2.2.(5.1), SS.C.1.2.5.(5.1), SS.D.1.2.1.(5.1), SS.D.2.2.4.(5.1)**	**Expository Writing – Report** The Three-fifths Compromise stated that three-fifths of the total number of slaves would be counted when figuring both representation to and taxes for the new United States government. Think about how this compromise affected both Northern and Southern states. Write a report explaining how the Three-fifths Compromise was good for both the North and the South under the new constitution.	► **TECHNOLOGY** Activity Book, p. 56	FCAT Practice Book, p. 34
SKILL Compromise to Resolve Conflicts p. 301	**SS.A.4.2.4.(5.1)** Knows the history of events and the historic figures responsible for historical documents important to the founding of the United States (for example, the Declaration of Independence, the United States Constitution, the Bill of Rights). **SS.A.4.2.4.(5.2)** Knows selected principal ideas expressed in significant historical documents important to the founding of the United States (including but not limited to the Declaration of Independence, the United States Constitution, the Bill of Rights, the Federalist Papers). **SS.C.1.2.1.(5.1)** Understands the functions of government under the framework of the United States constitution. **SS.A.1.2.2., SS.A.3.2.3**		Activity Book, p. 57 Transparency 25	
LESSON 4 A Government of Three Branches pp. 302–305 *(continued)*	**SS.C.1.2.1.(5.1)** Understands the functions of government under the framework of the United States constitution. **SS.C.1.2.1.(5.2)** Understands the branches of federal government and their main roles.	**Narrative Writing – Story** An idea for a new law is called a bill. Imagine that you are a bill being proposed by a member of Congress. Write a	Activity Book, p. 58 ► **DECISIONS, DECISIONS** ► **THE AMAZING WRITING MACHINE**	FCAT Practice Book, p. 35

	FLORIDA GRADE LEVEL EXPECTATIONS	FCAT WRITES	RESOURCES INCLUDING ▶ TECHNOLOGY	FCAT PRACTICE
(continued) **LESSON 4** **A Government of Three Branches** pp. 302–305	**SS.C.1.2.2.(5.1)** Understands the structure, functions, and primary responsibilities of executive, legislative, and judicial branches of the United States government. **SS.C.1.2.2.(5.2)** Understands ways all three branches of government promote the common good and protect individual rights. **SS.A.1.2.1.(5.1), SS.A.1.2.2, SS.A.3.2.3, SS.A.4.2.4.(5.1), SS.A.4.2.4.(5.2), SS.C.1.2.5.(5.1), SS.D.2.2.4.(5.1)**	story about the experiences you have as you try to become a law.		
LESSON 5 Learn History Through Literature 📖 **1787** by Joan Anderson illustrated by Teresa Fasolino pp. 306–311	**SS.A.1.2.1.(5.1)** Extends and refines understanding of the effects of individuals, ideas, and decisions on historical events (for example, in the United States). **SS.A.4.2.4.(5.1)** Knows the history of events and the historic figures responsible for historical documents important to the founding of the United States (for example, the Declaration of Independence, the United States Constitution, the Bill of Rights). **SS.A.4.2.4.(5.2)** Knows selected principal ideas expressed in significant historical documents important to the founding of the United States (including but not limited to the Declaration of Independence, the United States Constitution, the Bill of Rights, the Federalist Papers). **SS.C.1.2.1.(5.1)** Understands the functions of government under the framework of the United States constitution. **SS.A.1.2.3, SS.A.1.2.3.(5.1), SS.A.3.2.3, SS.C.1.2.1.(5.2), SS.C.1.2.2.(5.2), SS.C.1.2.5.(5.1)**	**Expository Writing – Explanation** Think about the arguments that members of the Constitutional Convention had both for and against a Bill of Rights. In the literature selection *1787*, Benjamin Franklin persuaded most delegates to put aside their differences and sign the constitution. Write a paragraph explaining why George Mason continued to refuse to sign the Constitution even after hearing Benjamin Franklin's plea.	Activity Book, p. 59 ▶ TIMELINER	FCAT Practice Book, p. 36
CHAPTER REVIEW pp. 312–313 *(continued)*	**SS.A.4.2.4.(5.1)** Knows the history of events and the historic figures responsible for historical documents important to the founding of the United States (for example, the Declaration of Independence, the United States Constitution, the Bill of Rights). **SS.A.4.2.4.(5.2)** Knows selected principal ideas expressed in significant historical documents important to the founding of the United States (including but not limited to the Declaration of Independence, the United States Constitution, the Bill of Rights, the Federalist Papers).		Activity Book, p. 60 Transparency 26 Chapter 9 Test, pp. 79–82 ▶ THE AMAZING WRITING MACHINE ▶ TIMELINER ▶ INTERNET	

Planning Chart

	FLORIDA GRADE LEVEL EXPECTATIONS	FCAT WRITES	RESOURCES INCLUDING ▶ TECHNOLOGY	FCAT PRACTICE
(continued) **CHAPTER REVIEW** pp. 312–313	**SS.B.1.2.1.(5.1)** Extends and refines use of maps, globes, charts, graphs, and other geographic tools including map keys and symbols to gather and interpret data and to draw conclusions about physical patterns (for example, in the United States). **SS.C.1.2.1.(5.1)** Understands the functions of government under the framework of the United States constitution. **SS.A.1.2.1.(5.1), SS.A.1.2.2, SS.A.1.2.3, SS.A.3.2.3, SS.B.1.2.2.(5.1), SS.C.1.2.1.(5.2), SS.C.1.2.2.(5.1), SS.C.1.2.2.(5.2), SS.C.1.2.5.(5.1), SS.D.1.2.1.(5.1)**			

Teacher's Notes

_____

_____

_____

_____

_____

_____

_____

Teacher's Notes

Planning Chart

	FLORIDA GRADE LEVEL EXPECTATIONS	FCAT WRITES	RESOURCES INCLUDING ► TECHNOLOGY	FCAT PRACTICE
LESSON 1 **Approving the Constitution** pp. 315–319	**SS.A.4.2.4.(5.1)** Knows the history of events and the historic figures responsible for historical documents important to the founding of the United States (for example, the Declaration of Independence, the United States Constitution, the Bill of Rights). **SS.A.4.2.4.(5.2)** Knows selected principal ideas expressed in significant historical documents important to the founding of the United States (including but not limited to the Declaration of Independence, the United States Constitution, the Bill of Rights, the Federalist Papers). **SS.C.1.2.1.(5.1)** Understands the functions of government under the framework of the United States constitution. **SS.A.1.2.1.(5.1), SS.A.1.2.2, SS.A.1.2.3, SS.A.3.2.3, SS.B.1.2.1.(5.1), SS.C.1.2.4.(5.1), SS.C.2.2.1.(5.1), SS.C.2.2.2.(5.1), SS.C.2.2.3.(5.1), SS.C.2.2.4.(5.1), SS.C.2.2.5.(5.1)**	**Narrative Writing – Story** Sam Adams went to the ratifying convention as a firm Anti-Federalist but returned home as a Federalist. Write a paragraph from his point of view in which he tells what he was thinking when he changed his mind about the Constitution.	Activity Book, p. 61	FCAT Practice Book, p. 37
COUNTERPOINTS **For or Against a Bill of Rights?** pp. 320–321	**SS.A.4.2.4.(5.1)** Knows the history of events and the historic figures responsible for historical documents important to the founding of the United States (for example, the Declaration of Independence, the United States Constitution, the Bill of Rights). **SS.A.4.2.4.(5.2)** Knows selected principal ideas expressed in significant historical documents important to the founding of the United States (including but not limited to the Declaration of Independence, the United States Constitution, the Bill of Rights, the Federalist Papers). **SS.C.2.2.5.(5.1)** Knows what constitutes personal, political, and economic rights and why they are important (for example, right to vote, assemble, lobby, own property and business). **SS.A.1.2.1.(5.1), SS.A.1.2.2, SS.A.1.2.3**			

TIME MANAGEMENT

DAY 1	DAY 2	DAY 3	DAY 4	DAY 5	DAY 6	DAY 7	DAY 8
Lesson 1	Counterpoints	Lesson 2	Lesson 3	Skill	Chapter Review	Chapter Test	Unit Wrap-Up

	FLORIDA GRADE LEVEL EXPECTATIONS	FCAT WRITES	RESOURCES INCLUDING	FCAT PRACTICE
LESSON 2 Rights and Responsibilities pp. 322–324	**SS.A.4.2.4.(5.1)** Knows the history of events and the historic figures responsible for historical documents important to the founding of the United States (for example, the Declaration of Independence, the United States Constitution, the Bill of Rights). **SS.A.4.2.4.(5.2)** Knows selected principal ideas expressed in significant historical documents important to the founding of the United States (including but not limited to the Declaration of Independence, the United States Constitution, the Bill of Rights, the Federalist Papers). **SS.C.2.2.1.(5.1)** Understands the importance of participation through community service, civic improvement, and political activities. **SS.C.2.2.3.(5.1)** Knows that a citizen is a legally recognized member of the United States who has certain rights and privileges and certain responsibilities (for example, privileges such as the right to vote and hold public office and responsibilities such as respecting the law, voting, paying taxes, serving on juries). **SS.A.1.2.1.(5.1), SS.A.1.2.3, SS.A.3.2.3, SS.B.1.2.1.(5.1), SS.C.1.2.1.(5.1), SS.C.1.2.2.(5.2), SS.C.2.2.2.(5.1), SS.C.2.2.4.(5.1), SS.C.2.2.5.(5.1)**	**Persuasive Writing – Opinion** In 1791 the Bill of Rights became a part of the United States Constitution. These ten amendments describe the freedoms that the government cannot take away and list actions the government is not allowed to take. Which of the first ten amendments to the Constitution do you think is the most important? Prepare notes for a short speech explaining your point of view.	▶ **TECHNOLOGY** Activity Book, p. 62	FCAT Practice Book, p. 38
LESSON 3 Putting the New Government to Work pp. 325–330	**SS.C.1.2.1.(5.1)** Understands the functions of government under the framework of the United States constitution. **SS.C.1.2.5.(5.1)** Knows basic things the United States government does in one's school, community, state, and nation. **SS.D.2.2.2.(5.1)** Understands the roles that money plays in a market economy. **SS.D.2.2.4.(5.1)** Knows ways the Federal government provides goods and services through taxation and borrowing (for example, highways, military defense). **SS.A.1.2.1.(5.1), SS.A.1.2.2, SS.A.1.2.3, SS.A.4.2.4.(5.2), SS.B.1.2.1.(5.1), SS.B.2.2.3.(5.1), SS.C.1.2.1.(5.2), SS.C.1.2.2.(5.1), SS.C.1.2.2.(5.2), SS.C.2.2.3.(5.1), SS.D.2.2.3.(5.1)**	**Expository Writing – Explanation** You are a member of Jefferson's Republican party. Write an article for a local newspaper explaining your party's "platform", or set of ideas in which it believes.	Activity Book, p. 63 Music Audiocassette ▶ **THE AMAZING WRITING MACHINE**	FCAT Practice Book, p. 39

Planning Chart

	FLORIDA GRADE LEVEL EXPECTATIONS	FCAT WRITES	RESOURCES INCLUDING	FCAT PRACTICE
SKILL **Learn from a Document** p. 331	**SS.A.1.2.2.(5.1)** Compares and contrasts primary and secondary accounts of selected historical events (for example, diary entries from a soldier in a Civil War battle and newspaper articles about the same battle). **SS.D.1.2.3.(5.1)** Understands the basic concept of credit. **SS.D.2.2.3.(5.1)** Understands basic services that banks and other financial institutions in the economy provide to consumers, savers, borrowers, and businesses. **SS.D.2.2.4.(5.1)** Knows ways the Federal government provides goods and services through taxation and borrowing (for example, highways, military defense). **SS.A.1.2.2, SS.A.1.2.3, SS.A.3.2.3, SS.C.1.2.1.(5.1), SS.C.1.2.1.(5.2), SS.C.1.2.2.(5.1), SS.C.1.2.2.(5.2), SS.C.1.2.5.(5.1), SS.D.2.2.2.(5.1)**		▶ **TECHNOLOGY** Activity Book, p. 64 Transparency 27	
CHAPTER REVIEW pp. 332–333	**SS.A.4.2.4.(5.1)** Knows the history of events and the historic figures responsible for historical documents important to the founding of the United States (for example, the Declaration of Independence, the United States Constitution, the Bill of Rights). **SS.A.4.2.4.(5.2)** Knows selected principal ideas expressed in significant historical documents important to the founding of the United States (including but not limited to the Declaration of Independence, the United States Constitution, the Bill of Rights, the Federalist Papers). **SS.C.1.2.1.(5.1)** Understands the functions of government under the framework of the United States constitution. **SS.C.2.2.3.(5.1)** Knows that a citizen is a legally recognized member of the United States who has certain rights and privileges and certain responsibilities (for example, privileges such as the right to vote and hold public office and responsibilities such as respecting the law, voting, paying taxes, serving on juries). **SS.A.1.2.1.(5.1), SS.C.1.2.1.(5.2), SS.C.1.2.2.(5.1), SS.C.1.2.2.(5.2), SS.C.1.2.5.(5.1), SS.C.2.2.1.(5.1), SS.C.2.2.5.(5.1)**		Activity Book, p. 65 Transparency 28 Assessment Program Chapter 10 Test, pp. 83–86 ▶ **THE AMAZING WRITING MACHINE** ▶ **TIMELINER** ▶ **INTERNET**	

	FLORIDA GRADE LEVEL EXPECTATIONS	FCAT WRITES	RESOURCES INCLUDING	FCAT PRACTICE
UNIT WRAP-UP Making Social Studies Relevant Visual Summary, Unit 5 Review pp. 334–339	**SS.A.4.2.4.(5.1)** Knows the history of events and the historic figures responsible for historical documents important to the founding of the United States (for example, the Declaration of Independence, the United States Constitution, the Bill of Rights). **SS.A.4.2.4.(5.2)** Knows selected principal ideas expressed in significant historical documents important to the founding of the United States (including but not limited to the Declaration of Independence, the United States Constitution, the Bill of Rights, the Federalist Papers). **SS.C.2.2.5.(5.1)** Knows what constitutes personal, political, and economic rights and why they are important (for example, right to vote, assemble, lobby, own property and business). **SS.D.1.2.1.(5.1)** Knows examples from United Sates history that demonstrate an understanding that all decisions involve opportunity costs and that making effective decisions involves considering the costs and the benefits associated with alternative choices. **SS.A.1.2.1.(5.1), SS.A.1.2.2, SS.A.1.2.3, SS.A.3.2.3, SS.B.1.2.1.(5.1), SS.C.1.2.1.(5.1), SS.C.1.2.1.(5.2), SS.C.1.2.2.(5.1), SS.C.1.2.2.(5.2), SS.C.1.2.4.(5.1), SS.C.1.2.5.(5.1), SS.C.2.2.1.(5.1), SS.C.2.2.2.(5.1), SS.C.2.2.3.(5.1), SS.C.2.2.4.(5.1), SS.C.2.2.5.(5.2)**		Making Social Studies Relevant Video Unit 5 Visual Summary Poster Game Time! Assessment Program Unit 5 Test, Standard Test, pp. 87–91 Performance Tasks, pp. 92–93 ▶ THE AMAZING WRITING MACHINE ▶ TIMELINER ▶ INTERNET	

Teacher's Notes

_____

_____

_____

Planning Chart

	FLORIDA GRADE LEVEL EXPECTATIONS	FCAT WRITES	RESOURCES INCLUDING	FCAT PRACTICE
UNIT INTRODUCTION Introduce the Unit Preview Set the Scene with Literature **Cassie's Journey** by Brett Harvey pp. 340–348	**SS.A.4.2.5.(5.1)** Understands selected geographic and economic features of growth and change that occurred in America from 1801 to 1861 (for example, the Lewis and Clark expedition, the Louisiana Purchase). **SS.A.4.2.5.(5.2)** Understands selected technological developments and their effects that occurred in America from 1801 to 1861 (for example, the cotton gin increasing the need for large numbers of slaves to pick cotton). **SS.B.1.2.1.(5.1)** Extends and refines use of maps, globes, charts, graphs, and other geographic tools including map keys and symbols to gather and interpret data and to draw conclusions about physical patterns (for example, in the United States). **SS.B.1.2.2.(5.1)** Knows how regions in the United States are constructed according to physical criteria and human criteria. **SS.A.1.21.(5.1), SS.A.1.2.2, SS.A.1.2.3, SS.A.3.2.1., SS.A.4.2.6.(5.1), SS.B.1.2.2.(5.1), SS.B.1.2.4, SS.B.2.2.1.(5.1), SS.B.2.2.2.(5.1), SS.C.1.2.1.(5.1), SS.C.2.2.3.(5.1), SS.C.2.2.5.(5.1), SS.D.1.2.1.(5.1), SS.D.1.2.2.(5.1)**		▶ **TECHNOLOGY** Unit 6 Visual Summary Poster Unit 6 Home Letter Unit 6 Text on Tape Audiocassette Video Experiences: Social Studies ▶ **TIMELINER**	

CHAPTER 11

	FLORIDA GRADE LEVEL EXPECTATIONS	FCAT WRITES	RESOURCES INCLUDING	FCAT PRACTICE
LESSON 1 **Across the Appalachians** pp. 349–352 *(continued)*	**SS.A.4.2.5.(5.1)** Understands selected geographic and economic features of growth and change that occurred in America from 1801 to 1861 (for example, the Lewis and Clark expedition, the Louisiana Purchase). **SS.B.1.2.2.(5.1)** Knows how regions in the United States are constructed according to physical criteria and human criteria. **SS.B.2.2.2.(5.1)** Understands ways the physical environment supports and constrains human activities in the United States.	**Expository Writing – Description** Most pioneer families had to be self-sufficient. They even had to build their own homes. Suppose that you were building your own home. What would it look like? How many rooms would it have? Now write two or three paragraphs describing your ideal home.	Activity Book, p. 66 ▶ **THE AMAZING WRITING MACHINE**	FCAT Practice Book, p. 40

TIME MANAGEMENT

DAY 1	DAY 2	DAY 3	DAY 4	DAY 5	DAY 6	DAY 7	DAY 8
Unit Introduction	Lesson 1	Lesson 2	Lesson 3	Skill	Lesson 4	Chapter Review	Chapter Test

	FLORIDA GRADE LEVEL EXPECTATIONS	FCAT WRITES	RESOURCES INCLUDING ▶ TECHNOLOGY	FCAT PRACTICE
(continued) **LESSON 1** **Across the Appalachians** pp. 349–352	**SS.D.1.2.2.(5.1)** Understands that scarcity of resources requires choices on many levels, from the individual to societal. **SS.A.1.2.1.(5.1), SS.A.1.2.2, SS.A.1.2.3, SS.A.4.2.5.(5.2), SS.B.1.2.1.(5.1), SS.B.1.2.4, SS.B.2.2.1.(5.1), SS.B.2.2.3.(5.1), SS.B.2.2.4, SS.D.1.2.1.(5.1), SS.D.2.2.1.(5.1)**			
LESSON 2 **The Louisiana Purchase** pp. 353–357	**SS.A.1.2.1.(5.1)** Extends and refines understanding of the effects of individuals, ideas, and decisions on historical events (for example, in the United States). **SS.A.1.2.2** The student uses a variety of methods and sources to understand history (e.g., interpreting diaries, letters, newspapers; and reading maps and graphs) and knows the difference between primary and secondary sources. **SS.A.4.2.5.(5.1)** Understands selected geographic and economic features of growth and change that occurred in America from 1801 to 1861 (for example, the Lewis and Clark expedition, the Louisiana Purchase). **SS.B.1.2.2.(5.1)** Knows how regions in the United States are constructed according to physical criteria and human criteria. **SS.A.1.2.3, SS.A.3.2.3, SS.B.1.2.1.(5.1), SS.B.2.2.2.(5.1), SS.C.1.2.1.(5.1), SS.C.1.2.2.(5.1), SS.D.1.2.1.(5.1), SS.D.1.2.2.(5.1), SS.D.1.2.5.(5.1), SS.D.2.2.1.(5.1), SS.D.2.2.2.(5.1)**	**Narrative Writing – Personal Experience** The section in your textbook about the Louisiana Purchase is titled "The Incredible Purchase". Think about something you have that was a "great buy." Then write a paragraph telling why it was an incredible purchase.	Activity Book, p. 67 ▶ THE AMAZING WRITING MACHINE	FCAT Practice Book, p. 41
LESSON 3 **A Second War with Britain** pp. 358–362 (continued)	**SS.A.4.2.5.(5.1)** Understands selected geographic and economic features of growth and change that occurred in America from 1801 to 1861 (for example, the Lewis and Clark expedition, the Louisiana Purchase). **SS.C.1.2.1.(5.1)** Understands the functions of government under the framework of the United States constitution. **SS.D.1.2.1.(5.1)** Knows examples from United States history that demonstrate an understanding that all decisions involve opportunity costs and that making effective decisions involves considering the costs and the benefits associated with alternative choices. **SS.D.1.2.2.(5.1)** Understands that scarcity of resources requires choices on many levels, from the individual to societal.	**Persuasive Writing – Speech** Upon hearing that a group of Indians was going to sell 3 million acres of land to the United States government, Tecumseh cried, "Sell a country! Why not sell the air, the clouds, and the great sea?" Imagine that you are Tecumseh. Write a speech that will persuade the Indians not to sell their land.	Activity Book, p. 68 ▶ THE AMAZING WRITING MACHINE	FCAT Practice Book, p. 42

Planning Chart

	FLORIDA GRADE LEVEL EXPECTATIONS	FCAT WRITES	RESOURCES INCLUDING ► TECHNOLOGY	FCAT PRACTICE
(continued) **LESSON 3** A Second War with Britain pp. 358–362	SS.A.1.2.1.(5.1), SS.A.1.2.2, SS.A.1.2.3, SS.B.1.2.1.(5.1), SS.B.1.2.2.(5.1), SS.C.1.2.1.(5.2), SS.C.1.2.2.(5.1), SS.C.1.2.2.(5.2), SS.C.1.2.5.(5.1)			
SKILL Predict a Likely Outcome p. 363	**SS.A.1.2.3** Understands broad categories of time in years, decades, and centuries. **SS.A.4.2.5.(5.1)** Understands selected geographic and economic features of growth and change that occurred in America from 1801 to 1861 (for example, the Lewis and Clark expedition, the Louisiana Purchase). **SS.B.1.2.2.(5.1)** Knows how regions in the United States are constructed according to physical criteria and human criteria. **SS.C.1.2.1.(5.1)** Understands the functions of government under the framework of the United States constitution. SS.A.1.2.1.(5.1), SS.A.3.2.3, SS.B.2.2.3.(5.1), SS.B.2.2.4, SS.C.1.2.1.(5.2), SS.C.1.2.2.(5.1), SS.C.1.2.2.(5.2), SS.C.1.2.5.(5.1)		Activity Book, p. 69 Transparency 29	
LESSON 4 Learn History Through Literature 📖 **By the Dawn's Early Light: The Story of The Star-Spangled Banner** by Steven Kroll illustrated by Dan Andreasen pp. 364–369	**SS.A.1.2.1.(5.1)** Extends and refines understanding of the effects of individuals, ideas, and decisions on historical events (for example, in the United States). **SS.A.1.2.2** The student uses a variety of methods and sources to understand history (e.g., interpreting diaries, letters, newspapers; and reading maps and graphs) and knows the difference between primary and secondary sources. **SS.A.4.2.5.(5.1)** Understands selected geographic and economic features of growth and change that occurred in America from 1801 to 1861 (for example, the Lewis and Clark expedition, the Louisiana Purchase). **SS.C.2.2.2.(5.1)** Extends and refines understanding of ways personal and civic responsibility are important. SS.A.1.2.3, SS.A.3.2.2, SS.B.1.2.1.(5.1), SS.C.1.2.1.(5.1), SS.C.1.2.2.(5.2)	**Narrative Writing – Song Lyrics** During the War of 1812, Francis Scott Key witnessed the British attack on Fort McHenry. He wrote "The Star-Spangled Banner" after seeing that the American flag was still flying. Think about a time when the person or group you were rooting for triumphed, for example, in a sporting event or a contest. Then, using "The Star-Spangled Banner" as a guide, write the lyrics for a song describing this victory.	Activity Book, p. 70 Music Audiocassette	FCAT Practice Book, p. 43

	FLORIDA GRADE LEVEL EXPECTATIONS	FCAT WRITES	RESOURCES INCLUDING	FCAT PRACTICE
CHAPTER REVIEW pp. 370–371	**SS.A.4.2.5.(5.1)** Understands selected geographic and economic features of growth and change that occurred in America from 1801 to 1861 (for example, the Lewis and Clark expedition, the Louisiana Purchase). **SS.A.4.2.5.(5.2)** Understands selected technological developments and their effects that occurred in America from 1801 to 1861 (for example, the cotton gin increasing the need for large numbers of slaves to pick cotton). **SS.B.1.2.2.(5.1)** Knows how regions in the United States are constructed according to physical criteria and human criteria. **SS.C.1.2.1.(5.1)** Understands the functions of government under the framework of the United States constitution. SS.A.1.2.1.(5.1), SS.A.3.2.3, SS.B.2.2.2.(5.1), SS.B.2.2.3.(5.1), SS.B.2.2.4, SS.C.1.2.1.(5.2), SS.C.1.2.2.(5.1), SS.C.1.2.2.(5.2), SS.C.2.2.2.(5.1), SS.D.1.2.1.(5.1), SS.D.1.2.2.(5.1)		▶ **TECHNOLOGY** Activity Book, p. 71 Transparency 30 Assessment Program Chapter 11 Test, pp. 95–98 ▶ THE AMAZING WRITING MACHINE ▶ TIMELINER ▶ INTERNET	

Teacher's Notes

_____

_____

_____

_____

_____

_____

_____

Planning Chart

	FLORIDA GRADE LEVEL EXPECTATIONS	FCAT WRITES	RESOURCES INCLUDING ► TECHNOLOGY	FCAT PRACTICE
LESSON 1 The Industrial Revolution pp. 373–378	**SS.A.4.2.5.(5.1)** Understands selected geographic and economic features of growth and change that occurred in America from 1801 to 1861 (for example, the Lewis and Clark expedition, the Louisiana Purchase). **SS.A.4.2.5.(5.2)** Understands selected technological developments and their effects that occurred in America from 1801 to 1861 (for example, the cotton gin increasing the need for large numbers of slaves to pick cotton). **SS.C.1.2.5.(5.1)** Knows basic things the United States government does in one's school, community, state, and nation. **SS.D.2.2.1.(5.1)** Understands economic specialization and how specialization generally affects costs, amount of goods and services produced, and interdependence. **SS.A.1.2.1.(5.1), SS.A.1.2.2, SS.B.1.2.1.(5.1), SS.B.1.2.2.(5.1), SS.B.1.2.4, SS.B.2.2.1.(5.1), SS.B.2.2.2.(5.1), SS.B.2.2.3.(5.1), SS.C.1.2.1.(5.1), SS.C.1.2.2.(5.2), SS.C.2.2.1.(5.1), SS.C.2.2.2.(5.1), SS.D.1.2.2.(5.1)**	**Expository Writing – Flow Chart** Eli Whitney invented a new way of manufacturing, called mass production, which could produce large amounts of goods at one time. Imagine that you have been put in charge of setting up a factory to manufacture your favorite game or toy. Create a flow chart showing the steps in the manufacturing process that will be necessary to produce this item.	Activity Book, p. 72 ► THE AMAZING WRITING MACHINE ► GRAPH LINKS ► DECISIONS, DECISIONS	FCAT Practice Book, p. 44
LESSON 2 The Age of Jackson pp. 379–382	**SS.A.4.2.5.(5.1)** Understands selected geographic and economic features of growth and change that occurred in America from 1801 to 1861 (for example, the Lewis and Clark expedition, the Louisiana Purchase). **SS.A.4.2.6.(5.1)** Understands selected economic and philosophical differences between the North and South prior to the Civil War, including but not limited to the institution of slavery. **SS.C.1.2.1.(5.1)** Understands the functions of government under the framework of the United States constitution.	**Narrative Writing – Poem** By 1838, United States soldiers had forced the last group of Cherokees to leave their lands and travel more than 800 miles to the Indian Territory. Along the way many Cherokees died of cold, disease, and lack of food. Write a poem about the Cherokee Trail of Tears to share with your class.	Activity Book, p. 73	FCAT Practice Book, p. 45

(continued)

TIME MANAGEMENT

DAY 1	DAY 2	DAY 3	DAY 4	DAY 5	DAY 6	DAY 7	DAY 8	DAY 9
Lesson 1	Lesson 2	Lesson 3	Skill	Lesson 4	Skill	Chapter Review	Chapter Test	Unit Wrap-Up

	FLORIDA GRADE LEVEL EXPECTATIONS	FCAT WRITES	RESOURCES INCLUDING ► TECHNOLOGY	FCAT PRACTICE
(continued) **LESSON 2** The Age of Jackson pp. 379–382	**SS.D.1.2.1.(5.1)** Knows examples from United Sates history that demonstrate an understanding that all decisions involve opportunity costs and that making effective decisions involves considering the costs and the benefits associated with alternative choices. **SS.A.1.2.1.(5.1), SS.B.1.2.1.(5.1), SS.B.1.2.2.(5.1), SS.B.1.2.5.(5.1), SS.B.2.2.2.(5.1), SS.C.1.2.1.(5.2), SS.C.1.2.2.(5.1), SS.C.1.2.5.(5.1), SS.C.2.2.3.(5.1), SS.C.2.2.4.(5.1), SS.D.2.2.4.(5.1)**			
LESSON 3 Westward Ho! pp. 383–389	**SS.A.1.2.3.(5.1)** Constructs and labels a timeline based on a historical reading (for example, about United States history). **SS.A.4.2.5.(5.1)** Understands selected geographic and economic features of growth and change that occurred in America from 1801 to 1861 (for example, the Lewis and Clark expedition, the Louisiana Purchase). **SS.A.4.2.5.(5.2)** Understands selected technological developments and their effects that occurred in America from 1801 to 1861 (for example, the cotton gin increasing the need for large numbers of slaves to pick cotton). **SS.D.1.2.1.(5.1)** Knows examples from United Sates history that demonstrate an understanding that all decisions involve opportunity costs and that making effective decisions involves considering the costs and the benefits associated with alternative choices. **SS.B.1.2.1.(5.1), SS.B.1.2.2.(5.1), SS.B.2.2.1.(5.1), SS.B.2.2.3.(5.1), SS.C.1.2.1.(5.2), SS.C.1.2.2.(5.1), SS.C.1.2.2.(5.2), SS.C.1.2.5.(5.1), SS.C.2.2.1.(5.1), SS.D.1.2.2.(5.1)**	**Expository Writing – Explanation** The journey over the Oregon Trail took six months and was full of hardship. Imagine that you are a pioneer journeying to a land you have never seen. You can take only five things with you on the trip. Decide what you will take. Then write a paragraph telling what these five things are and why you have chosen them.	Activity Book, p. 74 ► THE ALAMO ► THE AMAZING WRITING MACHINE ► NATIONAL INSPIRER ► TIMELINER	FCAT Practice Book, p. 46
SKILL Use Relief and Elevation Maps pp. 390–391 *(continued)*	**SS.A.1.2.2** Uses a variety of methods and sources to understand history (e.g., interpreting diaries, letters, newspapers; and reading maps and graphs) and knows the difference between primary and secondary sources. **SS.A.4.2.5.(5.1)** Understands selected geographic and economic features of growth and change that occurred in America from 1801 to 1861 (for example, the Lewis and Clark expedition, the Louisiana Purchase).		Activity Book, p. 75 Transparency 31 Desk Maps ► MAPSKILLS	

Planning Chart

	FLORIDA GRADE LEVEL EXPECTATIONS	FCAT WRITES	RESOURCES INCLUDING ▶ TECHNOLOGY	FCAT PRACTICE
(continued) **SKILL** Use Relief and Elevation Maps pp. 390–391	**SS.B.1.2.1.(5.1)** Extends and refines use of maps, globes, charts, graphs, and other geographic tools including map keys and symbols to gather and interpret data and to draw conclusions about physical patterns (for example, in the United States).			
LESSON 4 An Age of Reform pp. 392–396	**SS.A.4.2.5.(5.1)** Understands selected geographic and economic features of growth and change that occurred in America from 1801 to 1861 (for example, the Lewis and Clark expedition, the Louisiana Purchase). **SS.A.4.2.6.(5.1)** Understands selected economic and philosophical differences between the North and South prior to the Civil War, including but not limited to the institution of slavery. **SS.C.2.2.1.(5.1)** Understands the important of participation through community service, civic improvement, and political activities. **SS.C.2.2.3.(5.1)** Knows that a citizen is a legally recognized member of the United States who has certain rights and privileges and certain responsibilities (for example, privileges such as the right to vote and hold public office and responsibilities such as respecting the law, voting, paying taxes, serving on juries). **SS.A.1.2.1.(5.1), SS.A.1.2.2, SS.A.1.2.3, SS.B.1.2.1.(5.1), SS.C.2.2.2.(5.1), SS.C.2.2.5.(5.1)**	**Persuasive Writing – Opinion** Imagine that you are living in the mid-1800s. Horace Mann wants laws that will require children to go to school. What do you think of his idea? Write a letter to persuade the Board of Education to support your opinion.	Activity Book, p. 76 ▶ THE AMAZING WRITING MACHINE	FCAT Practice Book, p. 47
SKILL Use A Double-Bar Graph p. 397	**SS.A.4.2.5.(5.1)** Understands selected geographic and economic features of growth and change that occurred in America from 1801 to 1861 (for example, the Lewis and Clark expedition, the Louisiana Purchase). **SS.B.1.2.1.(5.1)** Extends and refines use of maps, globes, charts, graphs, and other geographic tools including map keys and symbols to gather and interpret data and to draw conclusions about physical patterns (for example, in the United States). **SS.B.1.2.2.(5.1)** Knows how regions in the United States are constructed according to physical criteria and human criteria. **SS.B.2.2.1.(5.1)** Understands reasons certain areas of the United States are more densely populated than others. **SS.A.1.2.2**		Activity Book, pp. 77–78 Transparency 32 ▶ GRAPH LINKS	

	FLORIDA GRADE LEVEL EXPECTATIONS	FCAT WRITES	RESOURCES INCLUDING	FCAT PRACTICE
CHAPTER REVIEW pp. 398–399	**SS.A.4.2.5.(5.1)** Understands selected geographic and economic features of growth and change that occurred in America from 1801 to 1861 (for example, the Lewis and Clark expedition, the Louisiana Purchase). **SS.A.4.2.5.(5.2)** Understands selected technological developments and their effects that occurred in America from 1801 to 1861 (for example, the cotton gin increasing the need for large numbers of slaves to pick cotton). **SS.B.1.2.1.(5.1)** Extends and refines use of maps, globes, charts, graphs, and other geographic tools including map keys and symbols to gather and interpret data and to draw conclusions about physical patterns (for example, in the United States). **SS.B.1.2.2.(5.1)** Knows how regions in the United States are constructed according to physical criteria and human criteria. **SS.A.1.2.1.(5.1), SS.A.1.2.2, SS.A.4.2.6.(5.1), SS.B.1.2.4, SS.B.2.2.2.(5.1), SS.B.2.2.3.(5.1), SS.C.2.2.1.(5.1), SS.C.2.2.2.(5.1), SS.C.2.2.3.(5.1), SS.C.2.2.5.(5.1), SS.D.1.2.1.(5.1)**		Activity Book, p. 79 Transparency 33 Assessment Program Chapter 12 Test, pp. 99–102 ▶ THE AMAZING WRITING MACHINE ▶ TIMELINER ▶ INTERNET	
UNIT WRAP-UP Making Social Studies Relevant Visual Summary Unit 6 Review pp. 400–405	**SS.A.1.2.3.(5.1)** Constructs and labels a timeline based on a historical reading (for example, about United States history). **SS.A.4.2.5.(5.1)** Understands selected geographic and economic features of growth and change that occurred in America from 1801 to 1861 (for example, the Lewis and Clark expedition, the Louisiana Purchase). **SS.A.4.2.5.(5.2)** Understands selected technological developments and their effects that occurred in America from 1801 to 1861 (for example, the cotton gin increasing the need for large numbers of slaves to pick cotton). **SS.B.1.2.2.(5.1)** Knows how regions in the United States are constructed according to physical criteria and human criteria. **SS.A.1.2.1.(5.1), SS.A.1.2.2, SS.A.1.2.3, SS.A.3.2.3, SS.A.4.2.6.(5.1), SS.A.5.2.7.(5.1), SS.B.1.2.1.(5.1), SS.B.1.2.4, SS.B.2.2.2.(5.1), SS.B.2.2.3.(5.1), SS.B.2.2.4, SS.C.1.2.1.(5.1), SS.C.1.2.5.(5.1), SS.C.2.2.1.(5.1), SS.C.2.2.5.(5.1), SS.D.1.2.1.(5.1)**		Making Social Studies Relevant Video Unit 6 Visual Summary Poster Game Time! Assessment Program Unit 6 Test, Standard Test, pp. 103–107 Performance Tasks, pp. 108–109 ▶ IMAGINATION EXPRESS ▶ THE AMAZING WRITING MACHINE ▶ TIMELINER ▶ INTERNET	

Planning Chart

	FLORIDA GRADE LEVEL EXPECTATIONS	FCAT WRITES	RESOURCES INCLUDING	FCAT PRACTICE
UNIT INTRODUCTION Introduce the Unit Preview Set the Scene with Literature **Stonewall** by Jean Fritz pp. 406–414	**SS.A.4.2.6.(5.1)** Understands selected economic and philosophical differences between the North and South prior to the Civil War, including but not limited to the institution of slavery. **SS.A.4.2.6.(5.2)** Knows roles and accomplishments of selected leaders on both side of the Civil War (for example, Abraham Lincoln, Ulysses Grant, Jefferson Davis, Robert E. Lee, Frederick Douglass, William Lloyd Garrison). **SS.A.4.2.6.(5.3)** Knows causes, selected key events, and effects of the Civil War (for example, major battles, the Emancipation Proclamation, General Lee's surrender at Appomattox Courthouse). **SS.B.1.2.1.(5.1)** Extends and refines use of maps, globes, charts, graphs, and other geographic tools including map keys and symbols to gather and interpret data and to draw conclusions about physical patterns (for example, in the United States). **SS.A.1.2.1.(5.1), SS.A.1.2.2, SS.A.1.2.3, SS.A.1.2.3.(5.1), SS.A.4.2.5.(5.1), SS.B.1.2.2.(5.1), SS.C.2.2.5.(5.1)**		▶ **TECHNOLOGY** Unit 7 Visual Summary Poster Unit 7 Home Letter Unit 7 Text on Tape Audiocassette Video Experiences: Social Studies ▶ **TimeLiner** ▶ **The Amazing Writing Machine**	

CHAPTER 13

	FLORIDA GRADE LEVEL EXPECTATIONS	FCAT WRITES	RESOURCES INCLUDING	FCAT PRACTICE
LESSON 1 Differences Divide North and South pp. 415–419	**SS.A.4.2.5.(5.1)** Understands selected geographic and economic features of growth and change that occurred in America from 1801 to 1861 (for example, the Lewis and Clark expedition, the Louisiana Purchase). **SS.A.4.2.5.(5.2)** Understands selected technological developments and their effects that occurred in America from 1801 to 1861 (for example, the cotton gin increasing the need for large numbers of slaves to pick cotton). **SS.A.4.2.6.(5.1)** Understands selected economic and philosophical differences between the North and South prior to the Civil War, including but not limited to the institution of slavery.	**Expository Writing – Compare and Contrast** In the mid-1800s, life was changing more rapidly for Americans living in the North than in the South. Look at the two paintings on page 416 of your textbook. Write a paragraph describing as many differences between life in a northern city and life on a southern plantation as you can find.	Activity Book, p. 80 ▶ **Graph Links**	FCAT Practice Book, p. 48

(continued)

TIME MANAGEMENT

DAY 1	DAY 2	DAY 3	DAY 4	DAY 5	DAY 6	DAY 7	DAY 8	DAY 9	DAY 10
Unit Introduction	Lesson 1	Skill	Lesson 2	Lesson 3	Lesson 4	Skill	Counterpoints	Chapter Review	Chapter Test

	FLORIDA GRADE LEVEL EXPECTATIONS	FCAT WRITES	RESOURCES INCLUDING ▶ TECHNOLOGY	FCAT PRACTICE
(continued) **LESSON 1** Differences Divide North and South pp. 415–419	**SS.A.4.2.6.(5.3)** Knows causes, selected key events, and effects of the Civil War (for example, major battles, the Emancipation Proclamation, General Lee's surrender at Appomattox Courthouse). **SS.A.1.2.1.(5.1), SS.A.1.2.2, SS.A.1.2.3, SS.A.3.2.1, SS.B.1.2.1.(5.1), SS.B.1.2.5.(5.1), SS.B.2.2.1.(5.1), SS.B.2.2.2.(5.1), SS.B.2.2.3.(5.1)**			
SKILL Use Graphs to Identify Trends p. 420	**SS.A.1.2.2** The student uses a variety of methods and sources to understand history (e.g., interpreting diaries, letters, newspapers; and reading maps and graphs) and knows the difference between primary and secondary sources. **SS.A.4.2.5.(5.1)** Understands selected geographic and economic features of growth and change that occurred in America from 1801 to 1861 (for example, the Lewis and Clark expedition, the Louisiana Purchase). **SS.A.4.2.6.(5.1)** Understands selected economic and philosophical differences between the North and South prior to the Civil War, including but not limited to the institution of slavery. **SS.B.2.2.2.(5.1)** Understands ways the physical environment supports and constrains human activities in the United States. **SS.A.1.2.3, SS.A.4.2.5.(5.2), SS.B.1.2.1.(5.1), SS.B.2.2.3.(5.1)**		Activity Book, p. 81 Transparency 34 ▶ GRAPH LINKS	
LESSON 2 Africans in Slavery and Freedom pp. 421–425 (continued)	**SS.A.4.2.6.(5.1)** Understands selected economic and philosophical differences between the North and South prior to the Civil War, including but not limited to the institution of slavery. **SS.A.4.2.6.(5.3)** Knows causes, selected key events, and effects of the Civil War (for example, major battles, the Emancipation Proclamation, General Lee's surrender at Appomattox Courthouse). **SS.B.1.2.1.(5.1)** Extends and refines use of maps, globes, charts, graphs, and other geographic tools including map keys and symbols to gather and interpret data and to draw conclusions about physical patterns (for example, in the United States). **SS.C.2.2.1.(5.1)** Understands the importance of participation through community service, civic improvement, and political activities.	**Narrative Writing – Travel Route** Imagine that you are a slave planning to escape from a plantation in Mississippi. Examine the map of the Underground Railroad on page 424 of your textbook. Which escape route would be the best one for you to take? What would you need to take with you? Write a paragraph about your plans for your escape to freedom.	Activity Book, p. 82 ▶ THE AMAZING WRITING MACHINE	FCAT Practice Book, p. 49

Planning Chart

	FLORIDA GRADE LEVEL EXPECTATIONS	FCAT WRITES	RESOURCES INCLUDING ▶ TECHNOLOGY	FCAT PRACTICE
(continued) **LESSON 2** Africans in Slavery and Freedom pp. 421–425	SS.A.1.2.2, SS.A.1.2.3, SS.A.3.2.3, SS.A.4.2.5.(5.1), SS.C.2.2.3.(5.1), SS.C.2.2.4.(5.1), SS.C.2.2.5.(5.1)			
LESSON 3 Facing a National Problem pp. 426–430	**SS.A.4.2.5.(5.1)** Understands selected geographic and economic features of growth and change that occurred in America from 1801 to 1861 (for example, the Lewis and Clark expedition, the Louisiana Purchase). **SS.A.4.2.6.(5.1)** Understands selected economic and philosophical differences between the North and South prior to the Civil War, including but not limited to the institution of slavery. **SS.A.4.2.6.(5.2)** Knows roles and accomplishments of selected leaders on both side of the Civil War (for example, Abraham Lincoln, Ulysses Grant, Jefferson Davis, Robert E. Lee, Frederick Douglass, William Lloyd Garrison). **SS.A.4.2.6.(5.3)** Knows causes, selected key events, and effects of the Civil War (for example, major battles, the Emancipation Proclamation, General Lee's surrender at Appomattox Courthouse). **SS.B.1.2.1.(5.1), SS.B.1.2.2.(5.1), SS.B.1.2.5.(5.1), SS.C.1.2.1.(5.1), SS.C.1.2.2.(5.2), SS.C.1.2.5.(5.1), SS.C.2.2.1.(5.1), SS.C.2.2.3.(5.1), SS.C.2.2.4.(5.1), SS.C.2.2.5.(5.1), SS.D.1.2.1.(5.1)**	**Persuasive Writing – Poster** In 1858, Abraham Lincoln entered a United States Senate race against Stephen A. Douglas. Which candidate would you want to help elect to the office of United States Senator? Design a campaign poster to help elect your favorite candidate. On your poster, be sure to describe the candidate's political platform and give reasons you think he should be elected.	Activity Book, p. 83 ▶ THE AMAZING WRITING MACHINE ▶ TIMELINER	FCAT Practice Book, p. 50
LESSON 4 A Time for Hard Decisions pp. 431–434 *(continued)*	**SS.A.4.2.6.(5.1)** Understands selected economic and philosophical differences between the North and South prior to the Civil War, including but not limited to the institution of slavery. **SS.A.4.2.6.(5.2)** Knows roles and accomplishments of selected leaders on both side of the Civil War (for example, Abraham Lincoln, Ulysses Grant, Jefferson Davis, Robert E. Lee, Frederick Douglass, William Lloyd Garrison). **SS.A.4.2.6.(5.3)** Knows causes, selected key events, and effects of the Civil War (for example, major battles, the Emancipation Proclamation, General Lee's surrender at Appomattox Courthouse).	**Expository Writing – Explanation** Abraham Lincoln and Jefferson Davis shared a goal in March of 1861. Each leader wanted to keep Fort Sumter under his control. Think about a time in your life when you had a goal. What did you plan to do? Write two or three paragraphs explaining what your goal was and the steps you took to achieve it.	Activity Book, p. 84 ▶ THE AMAZING WRITING MACHINE	FCAT Practice Book, p. 51

	FLORIDA GRADE LEVEL EXPECTATIONS	FCAT WRITES	RESOURCES INCLUDING ▶ TECHNOLOGY	FCAT PRACTICE
(continued) **LESSON 4** A Time for Hard Decisions pp. 431–434	**SS.D.1.2.1.(5.1)** Knows examples from United Sates history that demonstrate an understanding that all decisions involve opportunity costs and that making effective decisions involves considering the costs and the benefits associated with alternative choices. **SS.A.1.2.1.(5.1), SS.A.1.2.2, SS.A.1.2.3, SS.A.4.2.5.(5.1), SS.B.1.2.2.(5.1), SS.C.1.2.1.(5.1), SS.C.2.2.1.(5.1), SS.C.2.2.3.(5.1), SS.C.2.2.4.(5.1), SS.C.2.2.5.(5.1)**			
SKILL **Make a Thoughtful Decision** p. 435	**SS.A.1.2.2** Uses a variety of methods and sources to understand history (e.g., interpreting diaries, letters, newspapers; and reading maps and graphs) and knows the difference between primary and secondary sources. **SS.D.1.2.1.(5.1)** Knows examples from United Sates history that demonstrate an understanding that all decisions involve opportunity costs and that making effective decisions involves considering the costs and the benefits associated with alternative choices.		Activity Book, p. 85 Transparency 35	
COUNTERPOINTS **Union or Secession?** pp. 436–437	**SS.A.1.2.2** Uses a variety of methods and sources to understand history (e.g., interpreting diaries, letters, newspapers; and reading maps and graphs) and knows the difference between primary and secondary sources. **SS.A.4.2.6.(5.1)** Understands selected economic and philosophical differences between the North and South prior to the Civil War, including but not limited to the institution of slavery. **SS.D.1.2.1.(5.1)** Knows examples from United Sates history that demonstrate an understanding that all decisions involve opportunity costs and that making effective decisions involves considering the costs and the benefits associated with alternative choices.			
CHAPTER REVIEW pp. 438–439 (continued)	**SS.A.4.2.6.(5.1)** Understands selected economic and philosophical differences between the North and South prior to the Civil War, including but not limited to the institution of slavery. **SS.A.4.2.6.(5.3)** Knows causes, selected key events, and effects of the Civil War (for example, major battles, the Emancipation Proclamation, General Lee's surrender at Appomattox Courthouse).		Activity Book, p. 86 Transparency 36 Assessment Program Chapter 13 Test, pp. 111–114 ▶ THE AMAZING WRITING MACHINE ▶ TIMELINER	

Planning Chart

	FLORIDA GRADE LEVEL EXPECTATIONS	FCAT WRITES	RESOURCES INCLUDING	FCAT PRACTICE
(continued) **CHAPTER REVIEW** pp. 438–439	**SS.B.2.2.2.(5.1)** Understands ways the physical environment supports and constrains human activities in the United States. **SS.D.1.2.1.(5.1)** Knows examples from United Sates history that demonstrate an understanding that all decisions involve opportunity costs and that making effective decisions involves considering the costs and the benefits associated with alternative choices. **SS.A.1.2.3, SS.A.4.2.5.(5.1), SS.A.4.2.5.(5.2), SS.C.1.2.2.(5.2), SS.C.2.2.1.(5.1), SS.C.2.2.3.(5.1)**		▶ **TECHNOLOGY** ▶ **INTERNET**	

Teacher's Notes

Teacher's Notes

Planning Chart

	FLORIDA GRADE LEVEL EXPECTATIONS	FCAT WRITES	RESOURCES INCLUDING	FCAT PRACTICE
			▶ TECHNOLOGY	
LESSON 1 **The Fighting Begins** pp. 441–445	**SS.A.1.2.1.(5.1)** Extends and refines understanding of the effects of individuals, ideas, and decisions on historical events (for example, in the United States). **SS.A.4.2.6.(5.2)** Knows roles and accomplishments of selected leaders on both side of the Civil War (for example, Abraham Lincoln, Ulysses Grant, Jefferson Davis, Robert E. Lee, Frederick Douglass, William Lloyd Garrison). **SS.A.4.2.6.(5.3)** Knows causes, selected key events, and effects of the Civil War (for example, major battles, the Emancipation Proclamation, General Lee's surrender at Appomattox Courthouse). **SS.D.1.2.1.(5.1)** Knows examples from United Sates history that demonstrate an understanding that all decisions involve opportunity costs and that making effective decisions involves considering the costs and the benefits associated with alternative choices. **SS.A.1.2.2, SS.A.1.2.3, SS.B.1.2.1.(5.1), SS.B.1.2.2.(5.1), SS.C.2.2.1.(5.1), SS.C.2.2.2.(5.1), SS.C.2.2.3.(5.1), SS.C.2.2.4.(5.1)**	**Expository Writing – Biography** Clara Barton was a Union nurse during the Civil War. After the war ended, she continued to help others by founding the American Red Cross. Rose O'Neal Greenhow, Mary Surratt, Harriet Beecher Stowe, Belle Boyd, Harriet Tubman, and Sarah Edmonds are other well-known women of that time. Use your school library or the Internet to investigate one of these or another famous woman from the Civil War period. Then write a short biography about her life.	Activity Book, p. 87 ▶ THE AMAZING WRITING MACHINE ▶ MAPSKILLS	FCAT Practice Book, p. 52
LESSON 2 Learn History Through Literature **The Signature That Changed America** by Harold Holzer pp. 446–451	**SS.A.4.2.6.(5.2)** Knows roles and accomplishments of selected leaders on both side of the Civil War (for example, Abraham Lincoln, Ulysses Grant, Jefferson Davis, Robert E. Lee, Frederick Douglass, William Lloyd Garrison). **SS.A.4.2.6.(5.3)** Knows causes, selected key events, and effects of the Civil War (for example, major battles, the Emancipation Proclamation, General Lee's surrender at Appomattox Courthouse). **SS.C.1.2.2.(5.2)** Understands ways all three branches of government promote the common good and protect individual rights.	**Persuasive Writing – Letter** From the beginning of the Civil War, abolitionists urged Abraham Lincoln to issue an Emancipation Proclamation. However, for months Abraham Lincoln considered all points of view before declaring an order freeing the slaves. Imagine that you are an abolitionist. Write a letter to Lincoln to persuade him to issue	Activity Book, p. 88 ▶ THE AMAZING WRITING MACHINE	FCAT Practice Book, p. 53

(continued)

TIME MANAGEMENT

DAY 1	DAY 2	DAY 3	DAY 4	DAY 5	DAY 6	DAY 7	DAY 8
Lesson 1	Lesson 2	Lesson 3	Skill	Lesson 4	Chapter Review	Chapter Test	Unit Wrap-Up

	FLORIDA GRADE LEVEL EXPECTATIONS	FCAT WRITES	RESOURCES INCLUDING ▶ TECHNOLOGY	FCAT PRACTICE
(continued) **LESSON 2** Learn History Through Literature 📖 **The Signature That Changed America** by Harold Holzer pp. 446–451	**SS.C.2.2.5.(5.1)** Knows what constitutes personal, political, and economic rights and why they are important (for example, right to vote, assemble, lobby, own property and business). **SS.A.1.2.1.(5.1), SS.A.1.2.2, SS.A.1.2.3, SS.A.4.2.4.(5.1), SS.A.4.2.4.(5.2)**	the Emancipation Proclamation as soon as possible.		
LESSON 3 **The Long Road to a Union Victory** pp. 452–459	**SS.A.4.2.6.(5.2)** Knows roles and accomplishments of selected leaders on both side of the Civil War (for example, Abraham Lincoln, Ulysses Grant, Jefferson Davis, Robert E. Lee, Frederick Douglass, William Lloyd Garrison). **SS.A.4.2.6.(5.3)** Knows causes, selected key events, and effects of the Civil War (for example, major battles, the Emancipation Proclamation, General Lee's surrender at Appomattox Courthouse). **SS.D.1.2.1.(5.1)** Knows examples from United States history that demonstrate an understanding that all decisions involve opportunity costs and that making effective decisions involves considering the costs and benefits associated with alternative choices. **SS.D.1.2.2.(5.1)** Understands that scarcity of resources requires choices on many levels, from individual to societal. **SS.A.1.2.1.(5.1), SS.A.1.2.2, SS.A.4.2.4.(5.1), SS.A.4.2.4.(5.2), SS.B.1.2.1.(5.1), SS.B.1.2.2.(5.1), SS.C.2.2.1.(5.1), SS.C.2.2.2.(5.1), SS.C.2.2.3.(5.1), SS.C.2.2.4.(5.1)**	**Narrative Writing – Story** Create a character from the Civil War period, for example, a southern slave, a northern abolitionist, a Confederate soldier, a Union general, or a southern plantation owner. Write a story from the point of view of this character about the day Abraham Lincoln was assassinated.	Activity Book, p. 89 Music Audiocassette ▶ THE AMAZING WRITING MACHINE	FCAT Practice Book, p. 54
SKILL **Compare Maps with Different Scales** pp. 460–461	**SS.A.1.2.2** Uses a variety of methods and sources to understand history (e.g., interpreting diaries, letters, newspapers; and reading maps and graphs) and knows the difference between primary and secondary sources. **SS.A.1.2.3** Understands broad categories of time in years, decades, and centuries. **SS.A.4.2.6.(5.3)** Knows causes, selected key events, and effects of the Civil War (for example, major battles, the Emancipation Proclamation, General Lee's surrender at Appomattox Courthouse).		Activity Book, p. 90 Transparency 37 ▶ MAPSKILLS ▶ THE AMAZING WRITING MACHINE	

(continued)

Planning Chart

	FLORIDA GRADE LEVEL EXPECTATIONS	FCAT WRITES	RESOURCES INCLUDING ▶ TECHNOLOGY	FCAT PRACTICE
(continued) **SKILL** Compare Maps with Different Scales pp. 460–461	**SS.B.1.2.1.(5.1)** Extends and refines use of maps, globes, charts, graphs, and other geographic tools including map keys and symbols to gather and interpret data and to draw conclusions about physical patterns (for example, in the United States).			
LESSON 4 Life After the War pp. 462–467	**SS.A.4.2.6.(5.3)** Knows causes, selected key events, and effects of the Civil War (for example, major battles, the Emancipation Proclamation, General Lee's surrender at Appomattox Courthouse). **SS.A.4.2.6.(5.4)** Understands selected aspects of Reconstruction policies and ways they influenced the South after the Civil War. **SS.C.1.2.1.(5.1)** Understands the functions of government under the framework of the United States Constitution. **SS.D.2.2.4.(5.1)** Knows ways the Federal government provides goods and services through taxation and borrowing (for example, highways, military defense). **SS.A.4.2.4.(5.1), SS.A.4.2.4.(5.2), SS.A.4.2.6.(5.2), SS.B.1.2.2.(5.1), SS.B.2.2.2.(5.1), SS.C.1.2.5.(5.1), SS.C.2.2.3.(5.1), SS.C.2.2.4.(5.1), SS.C.2.2.5.(5.1), SS.D.1.2.1.(5.1), SS.D.1.2.2.(5.1)**	**Expository Writing – Newspaper Ad** After the Civil War and the passage of the Thirteenth Amendment to the Constitution, many former slaves began to search for family members who had been sold and sent away under slavery. Newspapers were filled with advertisements asking for help in finding loved ones. Imagine that you are a former slave and need to locate a missing family member or members. Write a newspaper ad that will help readers identify your lost relative.	Activity Book, p. 91 ▶ THE AMAZING WRITING MACHINE	FCAT Practice Book, p. 55
CHAPTER REVIEW pp. 468–469	**SS.A.4.2.6.(5.2)** Knows roles and accomplishments of selected leaders on both side of the Civil War (for example, Abraham Lincoln, Ulysses Grant, Jefferson Davis, Robert E. Lee, Frederick Douglass, William Lloyd Garrison). **SS.A.4.2.6.(5.3)** Knows causes, selected key events, and effects of the Civil War (for example, major battles, the Emancipation Proclamation, General Lee's surrender at Appomattox Courthouse). **SS.A.4.2.6.(5.4)** Understands selected aspects of Reconstruction policies and ways they influenced the South after the Civil War. **SS.B.1.2.1.(5.1)** Extends and refines use of maps, globes, charts, graphs, and other geographic tools including map keys and symbols to gather and interpret data and to draw conclusions about physical patterns (for example, in the United States).		Activity Book, p. 92 Transparency 38 Assessment Program Chapter 14 Test, pp. 115–118 ▶ THE AMAZING WRITING MACHINE ▶ TIMELINER ▶ INTERNET	

(continued)

	FLORIDA GRADE LEVEL EXPECTATIONS	FCAT WRITES	RESOURCES INCLUDING	FCAT PRACTICE
(continued) **CHAPTER REVIEW** pp. 462–469	SS.A.1.2.1.(5.1), SS.A.1.2.2, SS.A.4.2.4.(5.1), SS.A.4.2.4.(5.2), SS.B.1.2.2.(5.1), SS.C.1.2.2.(5.2), SS.C.1.2.5.(5.1), SS.C.2.2.5.(5.1), SS.D.1.2.1.(5.1), SS.D.1.2.2.(5.1), SS.D.2.2.4.(5.1)			
UNIT WRAP-UP *Making Social Studies Relevant* Visual Summary Unit 7 Review pp. 470–475	**SS.A.4.2.6.(5.1)** Understands selected economic and philosophical differences between the North and South prior to the Civil War, including but not limited to the institution of slavery. **SS.A.4.2.6.(5.2)** Knows roles and accomplishments of selected leaders on both side of the Civil War (for example, Abraham Lincoln, Ulysses Grant, Jefferson Davis, Robert E. Lee, Frederick Douglass, William Lloyd Garrison). **SS.A.4.2.6.(5.3)** Knows causes, selected key events, and effects of the Civil War (for example, major battles, the Emancipation Proclamation, General Lee's surrender at Appomattox Courthouse). **SS.A.4.2.6.(5.4)** Understands selected aspects of Reconstruction policies and ways they influenced the South after the Civil War. SS.A.1.2.1.(5.1), SS.A.1.2.2, SS.A.1.2.3, SS.A.1.2.3.(5.1), SS.B.1.2.1.(5.1), SS.B.1.2.2.(5.1), SS.B.2.2.2.(5.1), SS.B.2.2.3.(5.1), SS.B.2.2.4, SS.C.1.2.2.(5.2), SS.C.2.2.1.(5.1), SS.C.2.2.3.(5.1), SS.C.2.2.4.(5.1), SS.C.2.2.5.(5.1), SS.C.2.2.5.(5.2), SS.D.1.2.1.(5.1), SS.D.1.2.2.(5.1)		Making Social Studies Relevant Video Unit 7 Visual Summary Poster Game Time! Assessment Program Unit 7 Test, Standard Test, pp. 119–123 Performance Tasks, pp. 124–125 ▶ THE AMAZING WRITING MACHINE ▶ TIMELINER ▶ INTERNET	

Teacher's Notes

Planning Chart

	FLORIDA GRADE LEVEL EXPECTATIONS	FCAT WRITES	RESOURCES INCLUDING	FCAT PRACTICE
UNIT INTRODUCTION Introduce the Unit Preview Set the Scene with Literature **The Story of Thomas Alva Edison** by Margaret Cousins pp. 476–482	**SS.A.1.2.1.(5.1)** Extends and refines understanding of the effects of individuals, ideas, and decisions on historical events (for example, in the United States). **SS.A.5.2.1.(5.1)** Knows ways American life was transformed socially, economically, and politically after the Civil War. **SS.A.5.2.2.(5.1)** Knows selected economic, social, and political consequences of industrialization and urbanization in the United States after 1880 (for example, expansion of transportation, development of large population centers, woman's suffrage, rise of organized labor, improvements in the standard of living). **SS.B.1.2.1.(5.1)** Extends and refines use of maps, globes, charts, graphs, and other geographic tools including map keys and symbols to gather and interpret data and to draw conclusions about physical patterns (for example, in the United States). **SS.A.1.2.2, SS.A.1.2.3, SS.A.3.2.1, SS.B.1.2.4**		▶ **TECHNOLOGY** Unit 8 Visual Summary Poster Unit 8 Home Letter Unit 8 Text on Tape Audiocassette Video Experiences: Social Studies ▶ **TIMELINER**	
CHAPTER 15				
LESSON 1 **Big Business and Industrial Cities** pp. 483–487 (continued)	**SS.A.5.2.1.(5.1)** Knows ways American life was transformed socially, economically, and politically after the Civil War. **SS.A.5.2.2.(5.1)** Knows selected economic, social, and political consequences of industrialization and urbanization in the United States after 1880 (for example, expansion of transportation, development of large population centers, woman's suffrage, rise of organized labor, improvements in the standard of living). **SS.B.2.2.2.(5.1)** Understands ways the physical environment supports and constrains human activities in the United States.	**Expository Writing – Explanation** By 1899 John D. Rockefeller's Standard Oil Company had a monopoly, or almost complete control, of the oil business. Today the United States government has passed laws against creating unfair monopolies. Think about how a consumer can benefit from these laws. Then write a paragraph explaining two ways in which you are better off because of	Activity Book, p. 93 ▶ **LOOKING AHEAD! EARNING, SPENDING, SAVING** ▶ **THE AMAZING WRITING MACHINE**	FCAT Practice Book, p. 56

TIME MANAGEMENT

DAY 1	DAY 2	DAY 3	DAY 4	DAY 5	DAY 6	DAY 7	DAY 8	DAY 9	DAY 10
Unit Introduction	Lesson 1	Skill	Lesson 2	Lesson 3	Lesson 4	Lesson 5	Skill	Chapter Review	Chapter Test

10 DAYS

	FLORIDA GRADE LEVEL EXPECTATIONS	FCAT WRITES	RESOURCES INCLUDING	FCAT PRACTICE
(continued) **LESSON 1** Big Business and Industrial Cities pp. 483–487	**SS.D.2.2.1.(5.1)** Understands economic specialization and how specialization generally affects costs, amount of goods and services produced, and interdependence. **SS.A.1.2.1.(5.1), SS.A.1.2.2, SS.A.1.2.3, SS.B.1.2.1.(5.1), SS.B.1.2.2.(5.1), SS.B.2.2.1.(5.1), SS.B.2.2.3.(5.1), SS.B.2.2.4, SS.C.1.2.4.(5.1), SS.D.1.2.5.(5.2)**	laws that limit monopolies.that you are better off because of laws that limit monopolies.	► **TECHNOLOGY** Activity Book, p. 81 Transparenciy 34 ► **GRAPH LINKS**	
SKILL Use a Time Zone Map pp. 488–489	**SS.A.3.2.1** Knows significant people and their contributions in the field of communication and technology (e.g., inventors of various nonelectronic and electronic communication devices such as the steam engine and the television) and the impact of these devices on society. **SS.A.5.2.2.(5.1)** Knows selected economic, social, and political consequences of industrialization and urbanization in the United States after 1880 (for example, expansion of transportation, development of large population centers, woman's suffrage, rise of organized labor, improvements in the standard of living). **SS.B.1.2.1.(5.1)** Extends and refines use of maps, globes, charts, graphs, and other geographic tools including map keys and symbols to gather and interpret data and to draw conclusions about physical patterns (for example, in the United States). **SS.B.1.2.2.(5.1)** Knows how regions in the United States are constructed according to physical criteria and human criteria. **SS.A.1.2.1.(5.1), SS.A.1.2.2, SS.A.1.2.3, SS.B.1.2.4**		Activity Book, pp. 94–95 Transparency 39 ► **MAPSKILLS**	
LESSON 2 Growing Pains pp. 490–494	**SS.A.5.2.2.(5.1)** Knows selected economic, social, and political consequences of industrialization and urbanization in the United States after 1880 (for example, expansion of transportation, development of large population centers, woman's suffrage, rise of organized labor, improvements in the standard of living). **SS.C.1.2.4.(5.1)** Knows possible consequences of the absence of government, rules, and laws.	**Persuasive Writing – Letter** A labor union is a group of workers who take action to improve their working conditions. One union slogan was, "Eight hours for work, eight hours for rest, eight hours for what we will." Suppose you wanted to improve your working conditions by shortening	Activity Book, p. 96 ► **IMAGINATION EXPRESS**	FCAT Practice Book, p. 57
(continued)				

	FLORIDA GRADE LEVEL EXPECTATIONS	FCAT WRITES	RESOURCES INCLUDING ▶ TECHNOLOGY	FCAT PRACTICE
(continued) **LESSON 2** Growing Pains pp. 490–494	**SS.C.2.2.1.(5.1)** Understands the importance of participation through community service, civic improvement, and political activities. **SS.D.2.2.1.(5.1)** Understands economic specialization and how specialization generally affects costs, amount of goods and services produced, and interdependence. **SS.A.1.2.1.(5.1), SS.A.1.2.2, SS.A.1.2.3, SS.A.5.2.1.(5.1), SS.B.1.2.1.(5.1), SS.B.2.2.1.(5.1), SS.B.2.2.2.(5.1), SS.C.1.2.5.(5.1), SS.C.2.2.5.(5.1), SS.D.1.2.1.(5.1), SS.D.1.2.2.(5.1)**	the school day. Make up a slogan that expresses this idea. Then write a letter to persuade the school principal to carry out your idea.		
LESSON 3 New Immigrants pp. 495–499	**SS.A.5.2.1.(5.1)** Knows ways American life was transformed socially, economically, and politically after the Civil War. **SS.B.2.2.1.(5.1)** Understands reasons certain areas of the United States are more densely populated than others. **SS.C.2.2.3.(5.1)** Knows that a citizen is a legally recognized member of the United States who has certain rights and privileges and certain responsibilities (for example, privileges such as the right to vote and hold public office and responsibilities such as respecting the law, voting, paying taxes, servicing on juries). **SS.D.1.2.1.(5.1)** Knows examples from United States history that demonstrate an understanding that all decisions involve opportunity costs and that making effective decisions involves considering the costs and the benefits associated with alternative choices. **SS.A.1.2.2, SS.A.3.2.3, SS.A.5.2.2.(5.1), SS.B.1.2.1.(5.1), SS.B.1.2.2.(5.1), S.B.2.2.2.(5.1), SS.B.2.2.3.(5.1), SS.B.2.2.4, SS.C.1.2.5.(5.1), SS.C.2.2.4.(5.1), SS.D.1.2.2.(5.1)**	**Expository Writing – Explanation** Immigrants can become American citizens through a process called *naturalization*. Part of the naturalization process involves taking and passing a test about the United States. What sort of questions do you think should be on this test? Make a list of five questions. Write a paragraph explaining why you feel that these questions are important.	Activity Book, p. 97 ▶ THE AMAZING WRITING MACHINE	FCAT Practice Book, p. 58
LESSON 4 Learn History Through Literature **The Great Migration: An American Story** by Jacob Lawrence pp. 500–504 (continued)	**SS.A.5.2.1.(5.1)** Knows ways American life was transformed socially, economically, and politically after the Civil War. **SS.A.5.2.2.(5.1)** Knows selected economic, social, and political consequences of industrialization and urbanization in the United States after 1880 (for example, expansion of transportation, development of large population centers, woman's suffrage, rise of organized labor, improvements in the standard of living).	**Narrative Writing – Story** The lesson *The Great Migration: An American Story* ends with the sentence, "People all over the world are still on the move, trying to build better lives for themselves and for their families." Think about someone you know who has moved in order to	Activity Book, p. 98 ▶ THE AMAZING WRITING MACHINE	FCAT Practice Book, p. 59

	FLORIDA GRADE LEVEL EXPECTATIONS	FCAT WRITES	RESOURCES INCLUDING ▶ TECHNOLOGY	FCAT PRACTICE
(continued) **LESSON 4** Learn History Through Literature **The Great Migration: An American Story** by Jacob Lawrence pp. 500–504	**SS.C.2.2.5.(5.1)** Knows what constitutes personal, political, and economic rights and why they are important (for example, right to vote, assemble, lobby, own property and business). **SS.D.1.2.1.(5.1)** Knows examples from United States history that demonstrate an understanding that all decisions involve opportunity costs and that making effective decisions involves considering the costs and the benefits associated with alternative choices. **SS.A.1.2.1.(5.1), SS.A.1.2.3, SS.A.3.2.3, SS.B. 1.2.2.(5.1), SS.B.1.2.5.(5.1), SS.B.2.2.1.(5.1), SS.B.2.2.2.(5.1), SS.B.2.2.3.(5.1), SS.C. 2.2.3.(5.1), SS.D.1.2.2.(5.1), SS.D.2.2.1.(5.1)**	find a better life. This person could be a parent or grandparent, a neighbor, or someone in your school. Then write a short story telling about his or her part in The Great Migration.		
LESSON 5 **The Growth of Cities** pp. 505–508	**SS.A.5.2.1.(5.1)** Knows ways American life was transformed socially, economically, and politically after the Civil War. **SS.B.1.2.2.(5.1)** Knows how regions in the United States are constructed according to physical criteria and human criteria. **SS.B.2.2.1.(5.1)** Understands reasons certain areas of the United States are more densely populated than others. **SS.B.2.2.3.(5.1)** Understands ways human activity has affected the physical environment in various places and times in the United States. **SS.A.1.2.1.(5.1), SS.A.1.2.2, SS.A.1.2.3, SS.A.3.2.1, SS.A.5.2.2.(5.1), SS.C.1.2.4, SS.C.1.2.5.(5.1), SS.C.2.2.1.(5.1), SS.C.2.2.5.(5.1), SS.D.1.2.2.(5.1)**	**Persuasive Writing – Letter** Imagine that you live in an overcrowded tenement in the early 1900s. Insects and rats spread germs, garbage piles up, and there is great danger from fire and crime. Think about things that could be done to help improve these conditions. Then write a letter to the building's owner, describing the problems and persuading him or her to try your solutions.	Activity Book, p. 99	FCAT Practice Book, p. 60
SKILL **Solve a Problem** p. 509	**SS.A.5.2.1.(5.1)** Knows ways American life was transformed socially, economically, and politically after the Civil War. **SS.C.2.2.1.(5.1)** Understands the importance of participation through community service, civic improvement, and political activities. **SS.C.2.2.5.(5.1)** Knows what constitutes personal, political, and economic rights and why they are important (for example, right to vote, assemble, lobby, own property and business). **SS.D.1.2.2.(5.1)** Understands that scarcity of resources requires choices on many levels, from the individual to societal. **SS.B.1.2.2.(5.1), SS.B.2.2.1.(5.1)**		Activity Book, p. 100 Transparency 40	

Planning Chart

	FLORIDA GRADE LEVEL EXPECTATIONS	FCAT WRITES	RESOURCES INCLUDING	FCAT PRACTICE
CHAPTER REVIEW pp. 510–511	**SS.A.5.2.1.(5.1)** Knows ways American life was transformed socially, economically, and politically after the Civil War. **SS.A.5.2.2.(5.1)** Knows selected economic, social, and political consequences of industrialization and urbanization in the United States after 1880 (for example, expansion of transportation, development of large population centers, woman's suffrage, rise of organized labor, improvements in the standard of living). **SS.B.1.2.1.(5.1)** Extends and refines use of maps, globes, charts, graphs, and other geographic tools including map keys and symbols to gather and interpret data and to draw conclusions about physical patterns (for example, in the United States). **SS.B.1.2.2.(5.1)** Knows how regions in the United States are constructed according to physical criteria and human criteria. **SS.A.1.2.1.(5.1), SS.B.1.2.4, SS.B.2.2.1.(5.1), SS.B.2.2.2.(5.1), SS.B.2.2.3.(5.1), SS.C.2.2.1.(5.1), SS.C.2.2.3.(5.1), SS.C.2.2.5.(5.1), SS.D.1.2.1.(5.1), SS.D.1.2.2.(5.1), SS.D.2.2.1.(5.1)**		► **TECHNOLOGY** Activity Book, p. 101 Transparency 41 Assessment Program Chapter 15 Test, pp. 127–130 ► **THE AMAZING WRITING MACHINE** ► **TIMELINER** ► **INTERNET**	

Teacher's Notes

_____

_____

_____

_____

_____

Teacher's Notes

Planning Chart

	FLORIDA GRADE LEVEL EXPECTATIONS	FCAT WRITES	RESOURCES INCLUDING ► TECHNOLOGY	FCAT PRACTICE
LESSON 1 Farming the Great Plains pp. 513–517	**SS.A.5.2.1.(5.1)** Knows ways American life was transformed socially, economically, and politically after the Civil War. **SS.A.5.2.2.(5.1)** Knows selected economic, social, and political consequences of industrialization and urbanization in the United States after 1880 (for example, expansion of transportation, development of large population centers, woman's suffrage, rise of organized labor, improvements in the standard of living). **SS.B.2.2.3.(5.1)** Understands ways human activity has affected the physical environment in various places and times in the United States. **SS.D.2.2.1.(5.1)** Understands economic specialization and how specialization generally affects costs, amount of goods and services produced, and interdependence. **SS.A.1.2.1.(5.1), SS.A.1.2.2, S.A.1.2.3, SS.B.1.2.1.(5.1), SS.B.1.2.2.(5.1), SS.B.1.2.4, SS.B.2.2.1.(5.1), SS.B.2.2.2.(5.1), SS.C.1.2.2.(5.2), SS.C.1.2.5.(5.1), SS.D.1.2.1.(5.1), SS.D.1.2.2.(5.1)**	**Narrative Writing – Story** The Homestead Act opened the Great Plains to settlers. Imagine that you are a homesteader on the Great Plains in 1874 when a swarm of millions of grasshoppers attacks your farm. What can you do to protect your family and your farm? Write a story about what happens.	Activity Book, p. 102	FCAT Practice Book, p. 61
SKILL Understand a Climograph pp. 518–519	**SS.A.1.2.2** Used a variety of methods and sources to understand history (e.g., interpreting diaries, letters, newspapers; and reading maps and graphs) and knows the difference between primary and secondary sources. **SS.B.1.2.1.(5.1)** Extends and refines use of maps, globes, charts, graphs, and other geographic tools including map keys and symbols to gather and interpret data and to draw conclusions about physical patterns (for example, in the United States). **SS.B.1.2.5.(5.1)** Understands varying perceptions of regions throughout the United States.		Activity Book, p. 103 Transparency 42 ► GRAPH LINKS	

(continued)

TIME MANAGEMENT

DAY 1	DAY 2	DAY 3	DAY 4	DAY 5	DAY 6	DAY 7	DAY 8
Lesson 1	Skill	Lesson 2	Lesson 3	Lesson 4	Chapter Review	Chapter Test	Unit Wrap-Up

	FLORIDA GRADE LEVEL EXPECTATIONS	FCAT WRITES	RESOURCES INCLUDING ▶ TECHNOLOGY	FCAT PRACTICE
(continued) **SKILL** **Understand a Climograph** pp. 518–519	**SS.B.2.2.2.(5.1)** Understands ways the physical environment supports and constrains human activities in the United States.			
LESSON 2 **The Cattle Kingdom** pp. 520–524	**SS.A.5.2.1.(5.1)** Knows ways American life was transformed socially, economically, and politically after the Civil War. **SS.A.5.2.2.(5.1)** Knows selected economic, social, and political consequences of industrialization and urbanization in the United States after 1880 (for example, expansion of transportation, development of large population centers, woman's suffrage, rise of organized labor, improvements in the standard of living). **SS.B.1.2.4** Knows how changing transportation and communication technology have affected relationships between locations. **SS.D.2.2.1.(5.1)** Understands economic specialization and how specialization generally affects costs, amount of goods and services produced, and interdependence. SS.A.1.2.2, SS.A.1.2.3, SS.A.3.2.1, SS.B.1.2.1.(5.1), SS.B.1.2.2.(5.1), SS.B.1.2.5.(5.1), SS.B.2.2.3.(5.1), SS.B.2.2.4, SS.C.1.2.2.(5.2), SS.C.1.2.5.(5.1), SS.D.1.2.1.(5.1)	**Persuasive Writing – Television Commercial** In 1874 Joseph Glidden invented barbed wire. Think about the benefits of barbed wire for both ranchers and farmers. Then write a TV commercial to persuade viewers to purchase this new invention. Present your commercial to your class.	Activity Book, p. 104 Music Audiocassette	FCAT Practice Book, p. 62
LESSON 3 **Mining in the West** pp. 525–527	**SS.A.5.2.1.(5.1)** Knows ways American life was transformed socially, economically, and politically after the Civil War. **SS.B.2.2.1.(5.1)** Understands reasons certain areas of the United States are more densely populated than others. **SS.D.1.2.1.(5.1)** Knows examples from United States history that demonstrate an understanding that all decisions involve opportunity costs and that making effective decisions involves considering the costs and the benefits associated with alternative choices. **SS.D.1.2.2.(5.1)** Understands that scarcity of resources requires choices on many levels, from the individual to societal. SS.A.1.2.1.(5.1), SS.A.1.2.2, SS.A.1.2.3, SS.A.3.2.3, SS.A.5.2.2.(5.1), SS.B.1.2.1.(5.1), SS.B.1.2.2.(5.1), SS.B.2.2.3.(5.1), SS.B.2.2.4, SS.C.1.2.4.(5.1), SS.C.2.2.1.(5.1)	**Narrative Writing – Postcard** Gold miners rushed to the West after gold was discovered in the mid-1800s. Imagine that you are a prospector living in a mining town. Send a postcard to your family back home describing the town in which you live.	Activity Book, p. 105 ▶ **THE AMAZING WRITING MACHINE**	FCAT Practice Book, p. 63

Planning Chart

	FLORIDA GRADE LEVEL EXPECTATIONS	FCAT WRITES	RESOURCES INCLUDING	FCAT PRACTICE
LESSON 4 Conflict in the West pp. 528–531	**SS.A.5.2.1.(5.1)** Knows ways American life was transformed socially, economically, and politically after the Civil War. **SS.B.1.2.2.(5.1)** Knows how regions in the United States are constructed according to physical criteria and human criteria. **SS.C.2.2.5.(5.1)** Knows what constitutes personal, political, and economic rights and why they are important (for example, right to vote, assemble, lobby, own property and business). **SS.D.1.2.1.(5.1)** Knows examples from United States history that demonstrate an understanding that all decisions involve opportunity costs and that making effective decisions involves considering the costs and the benefits associated with alternative choices. **SS.A.1.2.3.(5.1)**, **SS.A.5.2.2.(5.1)**, **SS.B.1.2.1.(5.1)**, **SS.B.1.2.5.(5.1)**, **SS.B.2.2.1.(5.1)**, **SS.B.2.2.3.(5.1)**, **SS.C.1.2.2.(5.2)**, **SS.C.1.2.5.(5.1)**, **SS.C.2.2.3.(5.1)**, **SS.D.1.2.2.(5.1)**, **SS.D.2.2.1.(5.1)**	**Expository Writing – Telegram** After gold was discovered on the Great Sioux Reservation in 1875, thousands of miners invaded the Black Hills. This led to many disagreements and conflicts. In 1876 United States soldiers marched in to take the land. Imagine that you are a witness to the Battle of Little Bighorn. Write a telegram to President Grant describing Custer's defeat.	▶ **TECHNOLOGY** Activity Book, p. 106	FCAT Practice Book, p. 64
CHAPTER REVIEW pp. 532–533	**SS.A.5.2.1.(5.1)** Knows ways American life was transformed socially, economically, and politically after the Civil War. **SS.A.5.2.2.(5.1)** Knows selected economic, social, and political consequences of industrialization and urbanization in the United States after 1880 (for example, expansion of transportation, development of large population centers, woman's suffrage, rise of organized labor, improvements in the standard of living). **SS.D.1.2.2.(5.1)** Understands that scarcity of resources requires choices on many levels, from the individual to societal. **SS.D.2.2.1.(5.1)** Understands economic specialization and how specialization generally affects costs, amount of goods and services produced, and interdependence. **SS.A.1.2.1.(5.1)**, **SS.A.1.2.2**, **SS.B.1.2.1.(5.1)**, **SS.B.1.2.2.(5.1)**, **SS.B.1.2.5.(5.1)**, **SS.B.2.2.1.(5.1)**, **SS.B.2.2.2.(5.1)**, **SS.B.2.2.3.(5.1)**, **SS.C.1.2.2.(5.2)**, **SS.C.1.2.5.(5.1)**, **SS.D.1.2.1.(5.1)**		Activity Book, p. 107 Transparency 43 Assessment Program Chapter 16 Test, pp. 131–134 ▶ **THE AMAZING WRITING MACHINE** ▶ **TIMELINER** ▶ **INTERNET**	

FLORIDA GRADE LEVEL EXPECTATIONS	FCAT WRITES	RESOURCES INCLUDING	FCAT PRACTICE

UNIT WRAP-UP

Making Social Studies Relevant

Visual Summary

Unit 8 Review

pp. 534–539

SS.A.5.2.1.(5.1) Knows ways American life was transformed socially, economically, and politically after the Civil War.

SS.A.5.2.2.(5.1) Knows selected economic, social, and political consequences of industrialization and urbanization in the United States after 1880 (for example, expansion of transportation, development of large population centers, woman's suffrage, rise of organized labor, improvements in the standard of living).

SS.D.1.2.1.(5.1) Knows examples from United States history that demonstrate an understanding that all decisions involve opportunity costs and that making effective decisions involves considering the costs and the benefits associated with alternative choices.

SS.D.2.2.1.(5.1) Understands economic specialization and how specialization generally affects costs, amount of goods and services produced, and interdependence.

SS.A.1.2.1.(5.1), SS.A.1.2.2, SS.A.1.2.3, SS.A.3.2.1, SS.B.1.2.1.(5.1), SS.B.1.2.2.(5.1), SS.B.1.2.4, SS.B.2.2.1.(5.1), SS.B.2.2.2.(5.1), SS.B.2.2.3.(5.1), SS.B.2.2.4, SS.C.1.2.5.(5.2), SS.C.2.2.5.(5.1), SS.D.1.2.2.(5.1)

Making Social Studies Relevant Video

Unit 8 Visual Summary Poster

Game Time!

Assessment Program Unit 8 Test, Standard Test, pp. 135–139 Performance Tasks, pp. 140–141

▶ THE AMAZING WRITING MACHINE

▶ TimeLiner

▶ INTERNET

Teacher's Notes

_____

_____

_____

_____

Planning Chart

	FLORIDA GRADE LEVEL EXPECTATIONS	FCAT WRITES	RESOURCES INCLUDING	FCAT PRACTICE
UNIT INTRODUCTION Introduce the Unit Preview Set the Scene with Literature **This Man's War** by Charles F. Minder pp. 540–545	**SS.A.1.2.1.(5.1)** Extends and refines understanding of the effects of individuals, ideas, and decisions on historical events (for example, in the United States). **SS.A.5.2.3.(5.1)** Knows the political causes and outcomes of World War I (for example, isolationism, League of Nations). **SS.B.1.2.1.(5.1)** Extends and refines use of maps, globes, charts, graphs, and other geographic tools including map keys and symbols to gather and interpret data and to draw conclusions about physical patterns (for example, in the United States). **SS.C.2.2.2.(5.1)** Extends and refines understanding of ways personal and civic responsibility are important. **SS.A.1.2.2, SS.A.1.2.3, SS.A.5.2.4.(5.1), SS.A.5.2.5.(5.1), SS.A.5.2.6.(5.1), SS.A.5.2.6.(5.2), SS.B.2.2.3.(5.1), SS.B.2.2.4, SS.B.2.2.2.(5.1), SS.C.2.2.1.(5.1), SS.C.2.2.3.(5.1), SS.C.2.2.4.(5.1)**		▶ **TECHNOLOGY** Unit 9 Visual Summary Poster Unit 9 Home Letter Unit 9 Text on Tape Audiocassette Video Experiences: Social Studies ▶ **TIMELINER**	
CHAPTER 17				
LESSON 1 **Building an Empire** pp. 547–553	**SS.A.5.2.2.(5.1)** Knows selected economic, social, and political consequences of industrialization and urbanization in the United States after 1880 (for example, expansion of transportation, development of large population centers, woman's suffrage, rise of organized labor, improvements in the standard of living). **SS.B.2.2.2.(5.1)** Understands ways the physical environment supports and constrains human activities in the United States. **SS.C.1.2.1.(5.1)** Understands the functions of government under the framework of the United States Constitution.	**Persuasive Writing – Letter to the Editor** Leaders in the United States were accused of "imperialism" after they took control of Alaska and Hawaii. Imperialism is empire-building by gaining direct control of other countries or areas. Think about the areas claimed by the United States in the late 1800s and early 1900s. Then write a letter to the editor of a newspaper of that time to convince readers of the good points of imperialism.	Activity Book, p. 108	FCAT Practice Book, p. 65

(continued)

TIME MANAGEMENT

DAY 1	DAY 2	DAY 3	DAY 4	DAY 5	DAY 6	DAY 7	DAY 8
Unit Introduction	Lesson 1	Skill	Lesson 2	Lesson 3	Skill	Chapter Review	Chapter Test

	FLORIDA GRADE LEVEL EXPECTATIONS	FCAT WRITES	RESOURCES INCLUDING ▶ TECHNOLOGY	FCAT PRACTICE
(continued) **LESSON 1** **Building an Empire** pp. 547–553	**SS.D.1.2.1.(5.1)** Knows examples from United States history that demonstrate an understanding that all decisions involve opportunity costs and that making effective decisions involves considering the costs and the benefits associated with alternative choices. **SS.A.1.2.2., SS.B.1.2.1.(5.1), SS.B.1.2.2.(5.1), SS.B.2.2.3.(5.1), SS.C.1.2.1.(5.2), SS.C.1.2.2.(5.2), SS.C.1.2.5.(5.1), SS.C.2.2.1.(5.1), SS.C.2.2.2.(5.1), SS.C.2.2.3.(5.1), SS.C.2.2.4.(5.1), SS.C.2.2.5.(5.1)**			
SKILL **Compare Map Projections** pp. 554–555	**SS.A.1.2.2** Used a variety of methods and sources to understand history (e.g., interpreting diaries, letters, newspapers; and reading maps and graphs) and knows the difference between primary and secondary sources. **SS.A.5.2.2.(5.1)** Knows selected economic, social, and political consequences of industrialization and urbanization in the United States after 1880 (for example, expansion of transportation, development of large population centers, woman's suffrage, rise of organized labor, improvements in the standard of living). **SS.B.1.2.1.(5.1)** Extends and refines use of maps, globes, charts, graphs, and other geographic tools including map keys and symbols to gather and interpret data and to draw conclusions about physical patterns (for example, in the United States). **SS.B.1.2.2.(5.1)** Knows how regions in the United States are constructed according to physical criteria and human criteria. **SS.A.1.2.3**		Activity Book, pp. 109–110 Transparencies 44A–44B ▶ MAPSKILLS	
LESSON 2 **Progressives and Reform** pp. 556–558 *(continued)*	**SS.A.5.2.2.(5.1)** Knows selected economic, social, and political consequences of industrialization and urbanization in the United States after 1880 (for example, expansion of transportation, development of large population centers, woman's suffrage, rise of organized labor, improvements in the standard of living). **SS.C.1.2.2.(5.2)** Understands ways all three branches of government promote the common good and protect individual rights.	**Expository Writing – Itinerary** The first national park, Yosemite National Park, was established by the United States government in 1890. Think about a national park that you would like to visit. What would you like to do there? What would you like to see? Write an itinerary, or	Activity Book, p. 111	FCAT Practice Book, p. 66

Planning Chart

	FLORIDA GRADE LEVEL EXPECTATIONS	FCAT WRITES	RESOURCES INCLUDING ► TECHNOLOGY	FCAT PRACTICE
(continued) **LESSON 2** Progressives and Reform pp. 556–558	**SS.C.1.2.5.(5.1)** Knows basic things the United States government does in one's school, community, state, and nation. **SS.C.2.2.5.(5.1)** Knows what constitutes personal, political, and economic rights and why they are important (for example, right to vote, assemble, lobby, own property and business). **SS.A.1.2.3, SS.A.3.2.3, SS.B.2.2.3.(5.1), SS.B.2.2.4, SS.C.1.2.1.(5.2), SS.C.1.2.2.(5.1)**	outline, listing what you plan to do on your first visit to the park.		
LESSON 3 The Great War pp. 559–563	**SS.A.5.2.3.(5.1)** Knows the political causes and outcomes of World War I (for example, isolationism, League of Nations). **SS.B.1.2.2.(5.1)** Knows how regions in the United States are constructed according to physical criteria and human criteria. **SS.C.1.2.1.(5.1)** Understands the functions of government under the framework of the United States Constitution. **SS.C.2.2.2.(5.1)** Extends and refines understanding of ways personal and civic responsibility are important. **SS.A.1.2.1.(5.1), SS.B.1.2.1.(5.1), SS.B.2.2.3.(5.1), SS.C.1.2.1.(5.2), SS.C.1.2.2.(5.1), SS.C.1.2.2.(5.2), SS.C.1.2.5.(5.1), SS.C.2.2.1.(5.1), SS.C.2.2.3.(5.1), SS.C.2.2.4.(5.1)**	**Narrative Writing – Newspaper Article** On April 2, 1917, President Wilson asked the United States Congress to declare war on Germany. Write a headline and newspaper article announcing that the United States has entered World War I.	Activity Book, p. 112 Music Audiocassette ► TIMELINER	FCAT Practice Book, p. 67
SKILL Recognize Propaganda pp. 564–565	**SS.A.5.2.3.(5.1)** Knows the political causes and outcomes of World War I (for example, isolationism, League of Nations). **SS.C.1.2.5.(5.1)** Knows basic things the United States government does in one's school, community, state, and nation. **SS.D.1.2.1.(5.1)** Knows examples from United States history that demonstrate an understanding that all decisions involve opportunity costs and that making effective decisions involves considering the costs and the benefits associated with alternative choices. **SS.D.1.2.2.(5.1)** Understands that scarcity of resources requires choices on many levels, from the individual to societal. **SS.A.3.2.1, SS.A.3.2.3, SS.C.2.2.1.(5.1), SS.C.2.2.2.(5.1), SS.C.2.2.3.(5.1), SS.C.2.2.4.(5.1)**		Activity Book, p. 113 Transparency 45 ► THE AMAZING WRITING MACHINE	

GRADE 5

	FLORIDA GRADE LEVEL EXPECTATIONS	FCAT WRITES	RESOURCES INCLUDING	FCAT PRACTICE
CHAPTER REVIEW pp. 566–567	**SS.A.5.2.2.(5.1)** Knows selected economic, social, and political consequences of industrialization and urbanization in the United States after 1880 (for example, expansion of transportation, development of large population centers, woman's suffrage, rise of organized labor, improvements in the standard of living). **SS.A.5.2.3.(5.1)** Knows the political causes and outcomes of World War I (for example, isolationism, League of Nations). **SS.B.1.2.1.(5.1)** Extends and refines use of maps, globes, charts, graphs, and other geographic tools including map keys and symbols to gather and interpret data and to draw conclusions about physical patterns (for example, in the United States). **SS.C.1.2.1.(5.1)** Understands the functions of government under the framework of the United States Constitution. **SS.A.1.2.2, SS.C.1.2.2.(5.1), SS.D.1.2.1.(5.1)**		▶ **TECHNOLOGY** Activity Book, p. 114 Transparency 46 Assessment Program Chapter 17 Test, pp. 143–146 ▶ **THE AMAZING WRITING MACHINE** ▶ **TIMELINER** ▶ **INTERNET**	

Teacher's Notes

🖉🖉🖉🖉🖉🖉🖉🖉🖉🖉🖉🖉🖉🖉🖉🖉🖉🖉🖉🖉🖉🖉🖉🖉🖉🖉🖉🖉🖉

_____

_____

_____

_____

_____

_____

Planning Chart

	FLORIDA GRADE LEVEL EXPECTATIONS	FCAT WRITES	RESOURCES INCLUDING ▶ TECHNOLOGY	FCAT PRACTICE
LESSON 1 The Roaring Twenties pp. 569–573	**SS.A.3.2.1** Knows significant people and their contributions in the field of communication and technology (e.g., inventors of various nonelectronic and electronic communication devices such as the steam engine and the television) and the impact of these devices on society. **SS.A.5.2.4.(5.1)** Understands selected social and cultural transformations of the 1920's and 1930's (for example, impact of automobile, racial tensions, role of women). **SS.B.1.2.4** Knows how changing transportation and communication technology have affected relationships between locations. **SS.D.2.2.1.(5.1)** Understands economic specialization and how specialization generally affects costs, amount of goods and services produced, and interdependence. **SS.A.1.2.1.(5.1), SS.A.1.2.2, SS.A.1.2.3, SS.A.3.2.2, SS.B.1.2.2.(5.1), SS.B.1.2.5.(5.1), SS.D.1.2.2.(5.1)**	**Persuasive Writing – Speech** There were many achievements in the entertainment field during the 1920s. The first commercial radio stations began broadcasting, jazz music became popular, African American entertainers became well known, and talking movies were invented. Which of these achievements do you think had the greatest impact on today's society? Write a speech that would persuade others to agree with your opinion.	Activity Book, p. 115	FCAT Practice Book, p. 68
LESSON 2 The Great Depression and the New Deal pp. 574–578	**SS.A.5.2.4.(5.1)** Understands selected social and cultural transformations of the 1920's and 1930's (for example, impact of automobile, racial tensions, role of women). **SS.A.5.2.5.(5.1)** Understands social and economic impact of the Great Depression on American society (for example, business failures, unemployment, home foreclosures, breadlines). **SS.D.1.2.5.(5.2)** Knows different ways that money can increase in value through savings and investment (for example, bank savings accounts, stocks, bonds, real estate, other valuable goods). **SS.D.2.2.3.(5.1)** Understands basic services that banks and other financial institutions in the economy provide to consumers, savers, borrowers, and businesses.	**Narrative Writing – Story** The stock market crashed in 1929 and a long, difficult period called the Great Depression began. Look at the photograph of people waiting in a breadline on page 577 of your textbook. Imagine that you are one of the people in the photograph. Write a story telling how your life has changed because of the Great Depression.	Activity Book, p. 116	FCAT Practice Book, p. 69

(continued)

TIME MANAGEMENT

DAY 1	DAY 2	DAY 3	DAY 4	DAY 5	DAY 6	DAY 7	DAY 8	DAY 9
Lesson 1	Lesson 2	Lesson 3	Lesson 4	Lesson 5	Skill	Chapter Review	Chapter Test	Unit Wrap-Up

	FLORIDA GRADE LEVEL EXPECTATIONS	FCAT WRITES	RESOURCES INCLUDING ▶ TECHNOLOGY	FCAT PRACTICE
(continued) **LESSON 2** The Great Depression and the New Deal pp. 574–578	SS.A.1.2.1.(5.1), SS.A.1.2.2, SS.B.1.2.2.(5.1), SS.B.2.2.2.(5.1), SS.B.2.2.3.(5.1), SS.C.1.2.1.(5.1), SS.C.1.2.2.(5.1), SS.C.1.2.2.(5.2), SS.C.1.2.5.(5.1), SS.D.1.2.1.(5.1), SS.D.1.2.2.(5.1)			
LESSON 3 Learn History Through Literature 📖 **Children of the Dust Bowl** by Jerry Stanley pp. 579–582	**SS.A.5.2.5.(5.1)** Understands social and economic impact of the Great Depression on American society (for example, business failures, unemployment, home foreclosures, breadlines). **SS.B.2.2.2.(5.1)** Understands ways the physical environment supports and constrains human activities in the United States. **SS.D.1.2.2.(5.1)** Understands that scarcity of resources requires choices on many levels, from the individual to societal. **SS.D.2.2.3.(5.1)** Understands basic services that banks and other financial institutions in the economy provide to consumers, savers, borrowers, and businesses. SS.A.1.2.1.(5.1), SS.A.1.2.3, SS.A.5.2.4.(5.1), SS.B.1.2.2.(5.1), SS.B.2.2.3.(5.1), SS.C.1.2.1.(5.1), SS.C.1.2.2.(5.1), SS.C.1.2.2.(5.2), SS.C.1.2.5.(5.1), SS.D.1.2.1.(5.1)	**Expository Writing – Report** A drought that occurred in the Great Plains early in the 1930s changed the farmland to dry, dusty earth. Write a short report that describes living conditions in what became known as the Dust Bowl.	Activity Book, p. 117	FCAT Practice Book, p. 70
LESSON 4 World War II pp. 583–588	**SS.A.5.2.5.(5.1)** Understands social and economic impact of the Great Depression on American society (for example, business failures, unemployment, home foreclosures, breadlines). **SS.A.5.2.6.(5.1)** Understands selected events that led to the involvement of the United States in World War II (for example, German aggression in Eastern Europe, the bombing of Pearl Harbor). **SS.A.5.2.6.(5.2)** Understands selected causes, key events, people, and effects of World War II (for example, major battles such as the D-Day invasion, the dropping of the atomic bombs on Japan, reasons for the Allied victory, the Holocaust). **SS.D.1.2.1.(5.1)** Knows examples from United States history that demonstrate an understanding that all decisions involve opportunity costs and that making effective decisions involves considering the costs and the benefits associated with alternative choices.	**Persuasive Writing – Opinion** In February 1942 President Roosevelt ordered the army to put about 110,000 Japanese Americans into relocation camps. Do you believe this action was necessary? Write a paragraph to persuade readers to agree with your point of view.	Activity Book, p. 118 ▶ THE AMAZING WRITING MACHINE	FCAT Practice Book, p. 71
(continued)				

Planning Chart

	FLORIDA GRADE LEVEL EXPECTATIONS	FCAT WRITES	RESOURCES INCLUDING ▶ TECHNOLOGY	FCAT PRACTICE
(continued) **LESSON 4** World War II pp. 583–588	SS.A.1.2.1.(5.1), SS.B.1.2.1.(5.1), SS.C.1.2.1.(5.1), SS.C.1.2.2.(5.1), SS.C.1.2.2.(5.2), SS.C.1.2.5.(5.1), SS.C.2.2.1.(5.1), SS.C.2.2.2.(5.1), SS.C.2.2.5.(5.1), SS.D.1.2.2.(5.1), SS.D.2.2.1.(5.1)			
LESSON 5 The Allies Win the War pp. 589–594	**SS.A.5.2.6.(5.2)** Understands selected causes, key events, people, and effects of World War II (for example, major battles such as the D-Day invasion, the dropping of the atomic bombs on Japan, reasons for the Allied victory, the Holocaust). **SS.A.5.2.7.(5.1)** Knows selected economic, political, and social transformations which have taken place in the United States since World War II (for example, Civil Rights movement, role of women, Hispanic immigration, impact of new technologies, exploration of space). **SS.A.5.2.8.(5.1)** Knows selected political and military aspects of United States foreign relations since World War II (for example, Cold War attempts to contain communism such as in Berlin, Korea, Latin America, and Vietnam; nuclear weapons and the arms race; attempts to secure peace in the Middle East). **SS.D.1.2.1.(5.1)** Knows examples from United States history that demonstrate an understanding that all decisions involve opportunity costs and that making effective decisions involves considering the costs and the benefits associated with alternative choices. **SS.A.1.2.1.(5.1),** SS.A.1.2.2, SS.A.1.2.3, SS.A.3.2.3, SS.B. 1.2.1.(5.1), SS.B.1.2.2, SS.B.1.2.4, **SS.B.2.2.3.(5.1),** SS.B.2.2.4	**Narrative Writing – Letter** During World War II the Allies planned an invasion of Europe. On June 6, 1944, the date known as D day, the largest water-to-land invasion in history took place. Many soldiers died, but the invasion was successful. Imagine that you are a soldier who survived the battle. Write a letter home to your family describing this experience.	Activity Book, p. 119	FCAT Practice Book, p. 72
SKILL Read Parallel Time Lines p. 595	**SS.A.1.2.3.(5.1)** Constructs and labels a timeline based on a historical reading (for example, about United States history). **SS.A.5.2.6.(5.2)** Understands selected causes, key events, people, and effects of World War II (for example, major battles such as the D-Day invasion, the dropping of the atomic bombs on Japan, reasons for the Allied victory, the Holocaust). **SS.B.2.2.3.(5.1)** Understands ways human activity has affected the physical environment in various places and times in the United States.		Activity Book, p. 120 Transparency 47 ▶ TimeLiner	
(continued)				

	FLORIDA GRADE LEVEL EXPECTATIONS	FCAT WRITES	RESOURCES INCLUDING	FCAT PRACTICE
(continued) **SKILL** **Read Parallel Time Lines** p. 595	**SS.D.1.2.1.(5.1)** Knows examples from United States history that demonstrate an understanding that all decisions involve opportunity costs and that making effective decisions involves considering the costs and the benefits associated with alternative choices. **SS.A.1.2.3, SS.B.2.2.4**			
CHAPTER REVIEW pp. 596–597	**SS.A.5.2.4.(5.1)** Understands selected social and cultural transformations of the 1920's and 1930's (for example, impact of automobile, racial tensions, role of women). **SS.A.5.2.5.(5.1)** Understands social and economic impact of the Great Depression on American society (for example, business failures, unemployment, home foreclosures, breadlines). **SS.A.5.2.6.(5.1)** Understands selected events that led to the involvement of the United States in World War II (for example, German aggression in Eastern Europe, the bombing of Pearl Harbor). **SS.A.5.2.6.(5.2)** Understands selected causes, key events, people, and effects of World War II (for example, major battles such as the D-Day invasion, the dropping of the atomic bombs on Japan, reasons for the Allied victory, the Holocaust). **SS.A.1.2.1.(5.1), SS.A.5.2.7.(5.1), SS.A.5.2.8.(5.1), SS.B.1.2.1.(5.1), SS.B.2.2.3.(5.1), SS.C.1.2.2.(5.1), SS.C.1.2.2.(5.2), SS.D.1.2.1.(5.1), SS.D.1.2.3.(5.1), SS.D.2.2.1.(5.1), SS.D.2.2.3.(5.1)**		Activity Book, p. 121 Transparency 48 Assessment Program Chapter 18 Test, pp. 147–150 ▶ THE AMAZING WRITING MACHINE ▶ TIMELINER ▶ INTERNET	
UNIT WRAP-UP *Making Social Studies Relevant* Visual Summary Unit 9 Review pp. 598–603	**SS.A.5.2.4.(5.1)** Understands selected social and cultural transformations of the 1920's and 1930's (for example, impact of automobile, racial tensions, role of women). **SS.A.5.2.5.(5.1)** Understands social and economic impact of the Great Depression on American society (for example, business failures, unemployment, home foreclosures, breadlines). **SS.A.5.2.6.(5.1)** Understands selected events that led to the involvement of the United States in World War II (for example, German aggression in Eastern Europe, the bombing of Pearl Harbor).		Making Social Studies Relevant Video Unit 9 Visual Summary Poster Game Time! Assessment Program Unit 9 Test, Standard Test, pp. 151–155 Performance Tasks, pp. 156–157 ▶ THE AMAZING WRITING MACHINE ▶ TIMELINER ▶ INTERNET	
(continued)				

Planning Chart

	FLORIDA GRADE LEVEL EXPECTATIONS	FCAT WRITES	RESOURCES INCLUDING ▶ TECHNOLOGY	
(continued) **UNIT WRAP-UP** Making Social Studies Relevant Visual Summary Unit 9 Review pp. 598–603	**SS.A.5.2.7.(5.1)** Knows selected economic, political, and social transformations which have taken place in the United States since World War II (for example, Civil Rights movement, role of women, Hispanic immigration, impact of new technologies, exploration of space). **SS.A.1.2.3, SS.A.5.2.2.(5.1), SS.A.5.2.3.(5.1), SS.A.5.2.6.(5.2), SS.A.5.2.8.(5.1), SS.B.1.2.1.(5.1), SS.B.1.2.4, SS.B.2.2.3.(5.1), SS.C.2.2.1.(5.1), SS.C.2.2.3.(5.1), SS.C.2.2.5.(5.1), SS.D.1.2.2.(5.1), SS.D.2.2.1.(5.1), SS.D.2.2.3.(5.1)**			

Teacher's Notes

Teacher's Notes

Planning Chart

	FLORIDA GRADE LEVEL EXPECTATIONS	FCAT WRITES	RESOURCES INCLUDING	FCAT PRACTICE
UNIT INTRODUCTION Introduce the Unit Preview Set the Scene with Literature 📖 **On the Pulse of Morning** by Maya Angelou pp. 604–609	**SS.A.5.2.7.(5.1)** Knows selected economic, political, and social transformations which have taken place in the United States since World War II (for example, Civil Rights movement, role of women, Hispanic immigration, impact of new technologies, exploration of space). **SS.A.5.2.8.(5.1)** Knows selected political and military aspects of United States foreign relations since World War II (for example, Cold War attempts to contain communism such as in Berlin, Korea, Latin America, and Vietnam; nuclear weapons and the arms race; attempts to secure peace in the Middle East). **SS.B.1.2.1.(5.1)** Extends and refines use of maps, globes, charts, graphs, and other geographic tools including map keys and symbols to gather and interpret data and to draw conclusions about physical patterns (for example, in the United States). **SS.C.2.2.1.(5.1)** Understands the importance of participation through community service, civic improvement, and political activities. **SS.A.1.2.1.(5.1), SS.A.1.2.2, SS.A.1.2.3, SS.A.3.2.2, SS.B.1.2.2, SS.C.2.2.3.(5.1), SS.C.2.2.4.(5.1), SS.C.2.2.5.(5.1)**		► **TECHNOLOGY** Unit 10 Visual Summary Poster Unit 10 Home Letter Unit 10 Text on Tape Audiocassette Video Experiences: Social Studies	

CHAPTER 19

	FLORIDA GRADE LEVEL EXPECTATIONS	FCAT WRITES	RESOURCES INCLUDING	FCAT PRACTICE
LESSON 1 **The Cold War Begins** pp. 611–615 *(continued)*	**SS.A.5.2.7.(5.1)** Knows selected economic, political, and social transformations which have taken place in the United States since World War II (for example, Civil Rights movement, role of women, Hispanic immigration, impact of new technologies, exploration of space). **SS.A.5.2.8.(5.1)** Knows selected political and military aspects of United States foreign relations since World War II (for example, Cold War attempts to contain communism such as in Berlin, Korea, Latin America, and Vietnam; nuclear weapons and the arms race; attempts to secure peace in the Middle East).	**Persuasive Writing – Opinion** During the Cold War an arms race began between the Soviet Union and the United States. In an arms race one country builds weapons to protect itself against another country. The other country then builds even more weapons to protect itself. Think about whether this kind of race helps or hurts a country.	Activity Book, p. 122 ► **TimeLiner**	FCAT Practice Book, p. 73

TIME MANAGEMENT

DAY 1	DAY 2	DAY 3	DAY 4	DAY 5	DAY 6	DAY 7	DAY 8	DAY 9	DAY 10	DAY 11
Unit Introduction	Lesson 1	Lesson 2	Lesson 3	Skill	Lesson 4	Counterpoints	Lesson 5	Skill	Chapter Review	Chapter Test

	FLORIDA GRADE LEVEL EXPECTATIONS	FCAT WRITES	RESOURCES INCLUDING ▶ TECHNOLOGY	FCAT PRACTICE
(continued) **LESSON 1** **The Cold War Begins** pp. 611–615	**SS.B.1.2.2** Knows how regions are constructed according to physical criteria and human criteria. **SS.C.1.2.1.(5.1)** Understands the functions of government under the United States Constitution. **SS.A.1.2.1.(5.1), SS.A.1.2.2, SS.A.1.2.3, SS.A.3.2.3, SS.B.1.2.1.(5.1), SS.B.2.2.3.(5.1), SS.B.2.2.4, SS.C.1.2.2.(5.1), SS.C.1.2.5.(5.1), SS.C.2.2.3.(5.1), SS.C.2.2.5.(5.1), SS.D.1.2.1.(5.1)**	Then write a paragraph to persuade your classmates to support your opinion.		
LESSON 2 Learn History Through Literature **One Giant Leap** by Mary Ann Fraser pp. 616–621	**SS.A.1.2.1.(5.1)** Extends and refines understanding of the effects of individuals, ideas, and decisions on historical events (for example, in the United States). **SS.A.5.2.8.(5.1)** Knows selected political and military aspects of United States foreign relations since World War II (for example, Cold War attempts to contain communism such as in Berlin, Korea, Latin America, and Vietnam; nuclear weapons and the arms race; attempts to secure peace in the Middle East). **SS.B.2.2.2** Understands how the physical environment supports and constrains human activities. **SS.C.1.2.1.(5.1)** Understands the functions of government under the United States Constitution. **SS.A.1.2.2, SS.A.1.2.3, SS.B.2.2.3, SS.B.2.2.4**	**Narrative Writing – Script** On July 20, 1969, Neil Armstrong became the first person to set foot on the moon. A famous director wants you to make a movie about this historic moment and has hired you as the screenwriter. Write a page from the movie script. Be sure to set the scene and include dialogue between the characters.	Activity Book, p. 123 ▶ THE AMAZING WRITING MACHINE	FCAT Practice Book, p. 74
LESSON 3 **The Struggle for Equal Rights** pp. 622–626 *(continued)*	**SS.A.5.2.7.(5.1)** Knows selected economic, political, and social transformations which have taken place in the United States since World War II (for example, Civil Rights movement, role of women, Hispanic immigration, impact of new technologies, exploration of space). **SS.C.2.2.5.(5.1)** Knows what constitutes personal, political, and economic rights and why they are important (for example, right to vote, assemble, lobby, own property and business). **SS.C.2.2.5.(5.2)** Knows examples of contemporary issues regarding rights (for example, freedom from discrimination in housing, employment). **SS.D.1.2.2.(5.1)** Understands that scarcity of resources requires choices on many levels, from the individual to societal.	**Expository Writing – Letter** Many individuals made great contributions toward gaining civil rights for minorities and women. Among them were Rosa Parks, Thurgood Marshall, Dr. Martin Luther King, Jr., Malcolm X, César Chavez, Betty Friedan, and many others. Think about the person whose fight for civil rights you most admire. What would you say to him or her if you had the chance? Write a letter to that person, explaining	Activity Book, p. 124	FCAT Practice Book, p. 75

Planning Chart

	FLORIDA GRADE LEVEL EXPECTATIONS	FCAT WRITES	RESOURCES INCLUDING ▶ TECHNOLOGY	FCAT PRACTICE
(continued) **LESSON 3** The Struggle for Equal Rights pp. 622–626	SS.C.1.2.1.(5.1), SS.C.1.2.1.(5.2), SS.C.1.2.2.(5.1), SS.C.1.2.2.(5.2), SS.C.1.2.5.(5.1), SS.C.2.2.1.(5.1), SS.C.2.2.2.(5.1), SS.C.2.2.3.(5.1), SS.C.2.2.4.(5.1), SS.D.1.2.1.(5.1), SS.D.2.2.1.(5.1)	why you admire his or her struggle for civil rights.		
SKILL Act as a Responsible Citizen p. 627	**SS.A.5.2.7.(5.1)** Knows selected economic, political, and social transformations which have taken place in the United States since World War II (for example, Civil Rights movement, role of women, Hispanic immigration, impact of new technologies, exploration of space). **SS.C.2.2.1.(5.1)** Understands the importance of participation through community service, civic improvement, and political activities. **SS.C.2.2.4.(5.1)** Knows examples of the extension of the privileges and responsibilities of citizenship. **SS.C.2.2.5.(5.1)** Knows what constitutes personal, political, and economic rights and why they are important (for example, right to vote, assemble, lobby, own property and business). SS.A.1.2.1.(5.1), SS.C.2.2.2.(5.1), SS.C.2.2.3.(5.1), SS.C.2.2.5.(5.2), SS.D.1.2.2.(5.1)		Activity Book, p. 125 Transparency 49	
LESSON 4 Vietnam War and Protests at Home pp. 628–631	**SS.A.5.2.7.(5.1)** Knows selected economic, political, and social transformations which have taken place in the United States since World War II (for example, Civil Rights movement, role of women, Hispanic immigration, impact of new technologies, exploration of space). **SS.A.5.2.8.(5.1)** Knows selected political and military aspects of United States foreign relations since World War II (for example, Cold War attempts to contain communism such as in Berlin, Korea, Latin America, and Vietnam; nuclear weapons and the arms race; attempts to secure peace in the Middle East). **SS.C.2.2.1.(5.1)** Understands the importance of participation through community service, civic improvement, and political activities.	**Persuasive Writing – Speech for Television** Americans were divided in their opinion of the Vietnam War. Most leaders were either "Hawks" who supported the war, or "Doves" who wanted the war to end. How do you feel on the subject of whether the United States should have fought in the Vietnam War? Are you a Hawk or a Dove? Write a speech to present on television to persuade others to join your point of view.	Activity Book, p. 126	FCAT Practice Book, p. 76

(continued)

	FLORIDA GRADE LEVEL EXPECTATIONS	FCAT WRITES	RESOURCES INCLUDING ▶ TECHNOLOGY	FCAT PRACTICE
(continued) **LESSON 4** Vietnam War and Protests at Home pp. 628–631	**SS.D.1.2.1.(5.1)** Knows examples from United States history that demonstrate an understanding that all decisions involve opportunity costs and that making effective decisions involves considering the costs and the benefits associated with alternative choices. **SS.B.1.2.1.(5.1), SS.B.2.2.3.(5.1), SS.C.1.2.1.(5.1), SS.C.1.2.2.(5.1), SS.C.1.2.5.(5.1), SS.C.2.2.3.(5.1), SS.C.2.2.5.(5.1), SS.D.1.2.2.(5.1), SS.D.1.2.3.(5.1), SS.D.2.2.2.(5.1), SS.D.2.2.3.(5.1)**			
COUNTERPOINTS Hawk or Dove? pp. 632–633	**SS.A.1.2.2** Uses a variety of methods and sources to understand history (e.g., interpreting diaries, letters, newspapers; and reading maps and graphs) and knows the difference between primary and secondary sources. **SS.A.5.2.7.(5.1)** Knows selected economic, political, and social transformations which have taken place in the United States since World War II (for example, Civil Rights movement, role of women, Hispanic immigration, impact of new technologies, exploration of space). **SS.A.5.2.8.(5.1)** Knows selected political and military aspects of United States foreign relations since World War II (for example, Cold War attempts to contain communism such as in Berlin, Korea, Latin America, and Vietnam; nuclear weapons and the arms race; attempts to secure peace in the Middle East). **SS.C.1.2.2.(5.2)** Understands ways all three branches of government promote the common good and protect individual rights. **SS.A.1.2.1.(5.1), SS.A.1.2.3**			
LESSON 5 The Cold War Ends pp. 634–638 *(continued)*	**SS.A.5.2.7.(5.1)** Knows selected economic, political, and social transformations which have taken place in the United States since World War II (for example, Civil Rights movement, role of women, Hispanic immigration, impact of new technologies, exploration of space).	**Expository Writing – Explanation** In 1985, Mikhail Gorbachev became leader of the Soviet Union. He made many changes that gave people more of the freedoms they wanted. Think about the freedoms that you have living in the United States. Make a list of	Activity Book, p. 127 Music Audiocassette ▶ THE AMAZING WRITING MACHINE	FCAT Practice Book, p. 77

Planning Chart

	FLORIDA GRADE LEVEL EXPECTATIONS	FCAT WRITES	RESOURCES INCLUDING	FCAT PRACTICE
			▶ TECHNOLOGY	
(continued) **LESSON 5** The Cold War Ends pp. 634–638	**SS.A.5.2.8.(5.1)** Knows selected political and military aspects of United States foreign relations since World War II (for example, Cold War attempts to contain communism such as in Berlin, Korea, Latin America, and Vietnam; nuclear weapons and the arms race; attempts to secure peace in the Middle East). **SS.C.1.2.2.(5.2)** Understands ways all three branches of government promote the common good and protect individual rights. **SS.D.1.2.1.(5.1)** Knows examples from United States history that demonstrate an understanding that all decisions involve opportunity costs and that making effective decisions involves considering the costs and the benefits associated with alternative choices. **SS.A.1.2.1.(5.1), SS.A.1.2.2, SS.C.1.2.1.(5.1), SS.C.1.2.1.(5.2), SS.C.1.2.2.(5.1), SS.C.1.2.5.(5.1), SS.D.1.2.2.(5.1), SS.D.1.2.3.(5.1), SS.D.2.2.2.(5.1)**	these freedoms and explain why each one is important to you.		
SKILL Understand Political Symbols p. 639	**SS.A.1.2.2** Uses a variety of methods and sources to understand history (e.g., interpreting diaries, letters, newspapers; and reading maps and graphs) and knows the difference between primary and secondary sources. **SS.A.1.2.3** Understands broad categories of time in years, decades, and centuries. **SS.A.3.2.3** Understands the types of laws and government systems that have developed since the Renaissance (e.g., the development of democracy, the rise of totalitarian governments and dictatorships, communism and absolutism).		Activity Book, pp. 128–129 Transparency 50	
CHAPTER REVIEW pp. 640–641 *(continued)*	**SS.A.5.2.7.(5.1)** Knows selected economic, political, and social transformations which have taken place in the United States since World War II (for example, Civil Rights movement, role of women, Hispanic immigration, impact of new technologies, exploration of space). **SS.A.5.2.8.(5.1)** Knows selected political and military aspects of United States foreign relations since World War II (for example, Cold War attempts to contain communism such as in Berlin, Korea, Latin America, and Vietnam; nuclear weapons and the arms race; attempts to secure peace in the Middle East).		Activity Book, p. 130 Transparency 51 Assessment Program Chapter 19 Test, pp. 159–162 ▶ THE AMAZING WRITING MACHINE ▶ TIMELINER ▶ INTERNET	

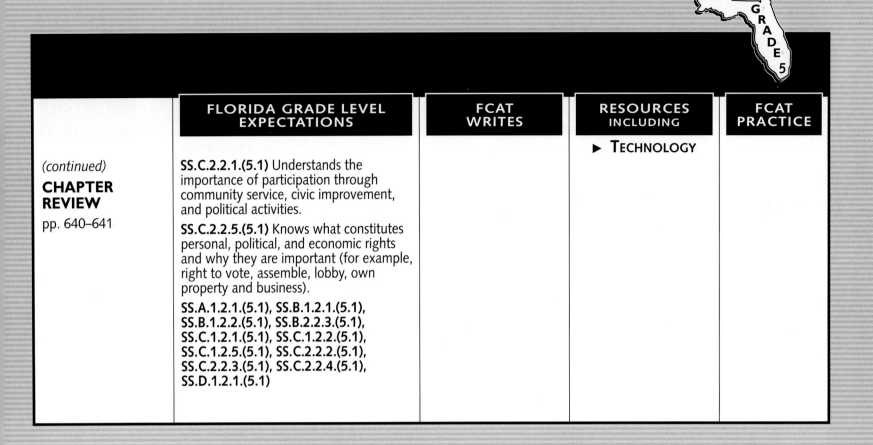

	FLORIDA GRADE LEVEL EXPECTATIONS	FCAT WRITES	RESOURCES INCLUDING ▶ TECHNOLOGY	FCAT PRACTICE
(continued) **CHAPTER REVIEW** pp. 640–641	**SS.C.2.2.1.(5.1)** Understands the importance of participation through community service, civic improvement, and political activities. **SS.C.2.2.5.(5.1)** Knows what constitutes personal, political, and economic rights and why they are important (for example, right to vote, assemble, lobby, own property and business). **SS.A.1.2.1.(5.1), SS.B.1.2.1.(5.1), SS.B.1.2.2.(5.1), SS.B.2.2.3.(5.1), SS.C.1.2.1.(5.1), SS.C.1.2.2.(5.1), SS.C.1.2.5.(5.1), SS.C.2.2.2.(5.1), SS.C.2.2.3.(5.1), SS.C.2.2.4.(5.1), SS.D.1.2.1.(5.1)**			

Teacher's Notes

_____

_____

_____

_____

_____

_____

_____

_____

Planning Chart

	FLORIDA GRADE LEVEL EXPECTATIONS	FCAT WRITES	RESOURCES INCLUDING ▶ TECHNOLOGY	FCAT PRACTICE
LESSON 1 Mexico Today pp. 643–646	**SS.A.5.2.8.(5.1)** Knows selected political and military aspects of United States foreign relations since World War II (for example, Cold War attempts to contain communism such as in Berlin, Korea, Latin America, and Vietnam; nuclear weapons and the arms race; attempts to secure peace in the Middle East). **SS.C.2.2.1.(5.1)** Understands the importance of participation through community service, civic improvement, and political activities. **SS.D.1.2.1** Understands that all decisions involve opportunity costs and that making effective decisions involves considering the costs and benefits associated with alternative choices. **SS.D.1.2.2.(5.1)** Understands that scarcity of resources requires choices on many levels, from the individual to societal. SS.A.1.2.2, SS.A.4.2.1.(5.2), SS.A.5.2.7.(5.1), SS.B.1.2.1.(5.1), SS.B.1.2.2.(5.1), SS.B.2.2.1, SS.B.2.2.2, SS.C.1.2.1.(5.1), SS.C.1.2.2.(5.1), SS.C.1.2.5.(5.1), SS.C.2.2.2.(5.1), SS.C.2.2.5.(5.1), SS.C.2.2.5.(5.2), SS.D.1.2.3.(5.1)	**Narrative Writing – Story** In the early 1500s, Tenochtitlán was destroyed when the Spanish conquered the Aztecs. Mexico City was built in its place. What might a citizen of Tenochtitlán think if he or she could see Mexico City today? What changes have taken place? Write a story that tells about an Aztec who suddenly finds himself or herself in downtown Mexico City.	Activity Book, p. 131 ▶ TIMELINER	FCAT Practice Book, p. 78
LESSON 2 Learn Culture Through Literature **Save My Rainforest** by Monica Zak pp. 647–651	**SS.A.1.2.2** Uses a variety of methods and sources to understand history (e.g., interpreting diaries, letters, newspapers; and reading maps and graphs) and knows the difference between primary and secondary sources. **SS.B.2.2.3** Understands how human activity affects the physical environment. **SS.B.2.2.4** Understands how factors such as population growth, human migration, improved methods of transportation and communication, and economic development affect the use and conservation of natural resources. **SS.D.1.2.2.(5.1)** Understands that scarcity of resources requires choices on many levels, from the individual to societal. SS.A.1.2.1.(5.1), SS.B.1.2.1.(5.1), SS.B.2.2.2	**Expository Writing – Web Page** Suppose that you were going to start an organization with the goal of saving the rain forest. Design a Web page for this organization. Be sure to include information explaining why it is important to preserve the rain forest. Then present ideas about how this can be done.	Activity Book, pp. 132–133 ▶ IMAGINATION EXPRESS	FCAT Practice Book, p. 79

90 DAYS

TIME MANAGEMENT

DAY 1	DAY 2	DAY 3	DAY 4	DAY 5	DAY 6	DAY 7	DAY 8	DAY 9
Lesson 1	Lesson 2	Skill	Lesson 3	Lesson 4	Lesson 5	Chapter Review	Chapter Test	Unit Wrap-Up

GRADE 5

	FLORIDA GRADE LEVEL EXPECTATIONS	FCAT WRITES	RESOURCES INCLUDING	FCAT PRACTICE
SKILL Use Population Maps pp. 652–653	**SS.A.1.2.2** Uses a variety of methods and sources to understand history (e.g., interpreting diaries, letters, newspapers; and reading maps and graphs) and knows the difference between primary and secondary sources. **SS.B.1.2.1.(5.1)** Extends and refines use of maps, globes, charts, graphs, and other geographic tools including map keys and symbols to gather and interpret data and to draw conclusions about physical patterns (for example, in the United States). **SS.B.1.2.2** Knows how regions are constructed according to physical criteria and human criteria. **SS.B.2.2.1** Understands why certain areas of the world are more densely populated than others.		▶ **TECHNOLOGY** Activity Book, pp. 134–135 Transparencies 52A–52B ▶ **MAPSKILLS**	
LESSON 3 Democracy in the Caribbean and in Central America pp. 654–658	**SS.A.1.2.3.(5.1)** Constructs and labels a timeline based on a historical reading (for example, about United States history). **SS.A.5.2.8.(5.1)** Knows selected political and military aspects of United States foreign relations since World War II (for example, Cold War attempts to contain communism such as in Berlin, Korea, Latin America, and Vietnam; nuclear weapons and the arms race; attempts to secure peace in the Middle East). **SS.C.2.2.1.(5.1)** Understands the importance of participation through community service, civic improvement, and political activities. **SS.D.1.2.2.(5.1)** Understands that scarcity of resources requires choices on many levels, from the individual to societal. **SS.A.1.2.1.(5.1), SS.C.1.2.1.(5.1), SS.C.2.2.2.(5.1), SS.C.2.2.3.(5.1), SS.C.2.2.4.(5.1), SS.D.1.2.1.(5.1)**	**Persuasive Writing – Opinion** In 1962 the United States established an embargo against Cuba. Do you think the United States should lift its embargo against Cuba? Why or why not? Write a paragraph to persuade your classmates to agree with your point of view.	Activity Book, pp. 136–137 ▶ **MAPSKILLS**	FCAT Practice Book, p. 80
LESSON 4 Challenges in South America pp. 659–661 *(continued)*	**SS.A.5.2.8.(5.1)** Knows selected political and military aspects of United States foreign relations since World War II (for example, Cold War attempts to contain communism such as in Berlin, Korea, Latin America, and Vietnam; nuclear weapons and the arms race; attempts to secure peace in the Middle East). **SS.B.2.2.2** Understands how the physical environment supports and constrains human activities. **SS.B.2.2.3** Understands how human activity affects the physical environment.	**Expository Writing – Speech** A problem for both South America and the United States is the production and sale of illegal drugs. Suppose you were the President of the United States. What would you do to control this problem? Write the speech you would make to the	Activity Book, pp. 138–139	FCAT Practice Book, p. 81

Planning Chart

	FLORIDA GRADE LEVEL EXPECTATIONS	FCAT WRITES	RESOURCES INCLUDING ▶ TECHNOLOGY	FCAT PRACTICE
(continued) **LESSON 4** Challenges in South America pp. 659–661	**SS.D.1.2.1** Understands that all decisions involve opportunity costs and that making effective decisions involves considering the costs and benefits associated with alternative choices. **SS.A.1.2.1.(5.1), SS.B.1.2.1.(5.1), SS.B.1.2.2, SS.C.1.2.1.(5.1), SS.C.2.2.1.(5.1), SS.C.2.2.2.(5.1), SS.C.2.2.5.(5.1), SS.C.2.2.5.(5.2), SS.D.1.2.2.(5.1), SS.D.2.2.1.(5.1)**	American people describing your plan to stop the sale and use of illegal drugs in the United States.		
LESSON 5 The Peoples of Canada pp. 662–665	**SS.B.1.2.2** Knows how regions are constructed according to physical criteria and human criteria. **SS.C.2.2.1.(5.1)** Understands the importance of participation through community service, civic improvement, and political activities. **SS.C.2.2.5.(5.1)** Knows what constitutes personal, political, and economic rights and why they are important (for example, right to vote, assemble, lobby, own property and business). **SS.C.2.2.5.(5.2)** Knows examples of contemporary issues regarding rights (for example, freedom from discrimination in housing, employment). **SS.A.1.2.2, SS.A.1.2.3, SS.A.4.2.1.(5.2), SS.B.1.2.1.(5.1), SS.B.2.2.2, SS.B.2.2.3, SS.C.2.2.2.(5.1), SS.D.1.2.1, SS.D.1.2.2.(5.1)**	**Expository Writing – Compare and Contrast** Canada is the second-largest country in the world. Think about the heritage and beliefs of both the Québecois separatists and the Canadian Indians. Then write a paper comparing and contrasting the two groups.	Activity Book, pp. 140–141 ▶ GRAPH LINKS	FCAT Practice Book, p. 82
CHAPTER REVIEW pp. 666–667 (continued)	**SS.A.5.2.8.(5.1)** Knows selected political and military aspects of United States foreign relations since World War II (for example, Cold War attempts to contain communism such as in Berlin, Korea, Latin America, and Vietnam; nuclear weapons and the arms race; attempts to secure peace in the Middle East). **SS.B.1.2.1.(5.1)** Extends and refines use of maps, globes, charts, graphs, and other geographic tools including map keys and symbols to gather and interpret data and to draw conclusions about physical patterns (for example, in the United States). **SS.C.2.2.1.(5.1)** Understands the importance of participation through community service, civic improvement, and political activities. **SS.D.1.2.1** Understands that all decisions involve opportunity costs and that making effective decisions involves considering the costs and benefits associated with alternative choices.		Activity Book, p. 142 Transparency 53 Assessment Program Chapter 20 Test, pp. 163–166 ▶ THE AMAZING WRITING MACHINE ▶ TIMELINER ▶ INTERNET	

	FLORIDA GRADE LEVEL EXPECTATIONS	FCAT WRITES	RESOURCES INCLUDING	FCAT PRACTICE
(continued) **CHAPTER REVIEW** pp. 666–667	SS.B.2.2.1, SS.B.2.2.2, SS.B.2.2.3, SS.C.1.2.1.(5.1), SS.C.1.2.2.(5.1), SS.C.1.2.5.(5.1), SS.C.2.2.2.(5.1), S.C.2.2.3.(5.1), SS.C.2.2.5.(5.1), SS.D.1.2.2.(5.1), SS.D.2.2.2.(5.1)			
UNIT WRAP-UP Making Social Studies Relevant Visual Summary Unit 10 Review pp. 668–673	**SS.A.5.2.7.(5.1)** Knows selected economic, political, and social transformations which have taken place in the United States since World War II (for example, Civil Rights movement, role of women, Hispanic immigration, impact of new technologies, exploration of space). **SS.A.5.2.8.(5.1)** Knows selected political and military aspects of United States foreign relations since World War II (for example, Cold War attempts to contain communism such as in Berlin, Korea, Latin America, and Vietnam; nuclear weapons and the arms race; attempts to secure peace in the Middle East). **SS.B.1.2.2** Knows how regions are constructed according to physical criteria and human criteria. **SS.C.2.2.1.(5.1)** Understands the importance of participation through community service, civic improvement, and political activities. SS.A.1.2.1.(5.1), SS.A.1.2.2, SS.A.1.2.3, SS.A.3.2.3, SS.B.1.2.1.(5.1), SS.B.2.2.1.(5.1), SS.B.2.2.2, SS.B.2.2.3, SS.B.2.2.4, SS.C.1.2.1.(5.1), SS.C.1.2.5.(5.1), SS.D.1.2.1.(5.1), SS.D.1.2.2.(5.1), SS.D.2.2.1.(5.1), SS.D.2.2.2.(5.1)		Making Social Studies Relevant Video Unit 10 Visual Summary Poster Game Time! Assessment Program Unit 10 Test, Standard Test, pp. 167–171 Performance Tasks, pp. 172–173 ► THE AMAZING WRITING MACHINE ► TIMELINER ► INTERNET	

Teacher's Notes

_____

_____

_____

Sunshine State Standards
Grade Level Expectations
Social Studies
Fifth Grade

A. TIME, CONTINUITY, AND CHANGE (History)

1. **The student understands historical chronology and the historical perspective.**

   SS.A.1.2.1 understands how individuals, ideas, decisions, and events can influence history

   - **SS.A.1.2.1.(5.1)** extends and refines understanding of the effects of individuals, ideas, and decisions on historical events (for example, in the United States)

   SS.A.1.2.2 uses a variety of methods and sources to understand history (for example, interpreting diaries, letters, newspapers; and reading maps and graphs) and knows the difference between primary and secondary sources

   - **SS.A.1.2.2.(5.1)** compares and contrasts primary and secondary accounts of selected historical events (for example, diary entries from a soldier in a Civil War battle and newspaper articles about the same battle)

   SS.A.1.2.3 understands broad categories of time in years, decades, and centuries

   - **SS.A.1.2.3.(5.1)** constructs and labels a timeline based on a historical reading (for example, about United States history)

2. **The student understands the world from its beginnings to the time of the Renaissance.**

   SS.A.2.2.1 knows the significant scientific and technological achievements of various societies (for example, the invention of paper in China, Mayan calendars, mummification and the use of cotton in Egypt, astronomical discoveries in the Moslem world, and the Arabic number system)

   - content addressed in third grade

   SS.A.2.2.2 understands developments in transportation and communication in various societies (for example, the development of extensive road systems in various cultures, the difficulties of travel and communication encountered by people of various cultures, the origins and changes in writing and how these changes made communication between people more effective)

   - content addressed in third grade

   SS.A.2.2.3 understands various aspects of family life, structures, and roles in different cultures and in many eras (for example, pastoral and agrarian families of early civilizations, families of ancient times, and medieval families)

   - content addressed in third grade

   SS.A.2.2.4 understands the emergence of different laws and systems of government (for example, monarchy and republic)

   - content addressed in third grade

SS.A.2.2.5 understands significant achievements in the humanities to the time of the Renaissance (for example, Roman architecture and Greek art)

- content addressed in third grade

SS.A.2.2.6 knows how trade led to exploration in other regions of the world (for example, the explorations of Marco Polo and the Vikings)

- content addressed in third grade

SS.A.2.2.7 understands how developments in the Middle Ages contributed to modern life (for example, the development of social institutions and organizations, the rise of cities, the formation of guilds, the rise of commerce, the influence of the church, and the rise of universities)

- content addressed in third grade

3. **The student understands Western and Eastern civilization since the Renaissance.**

SS.A.3.2.1 knows significant people and their contributions in the fields of communication and technology (for example, inventors of various nonelectronic and electronic communication devices such as the steam engine and the television) and the impact of these devices on society

- content addressed in United States history (SS.A.4.2.1-8)

SS.A.3.2.2 knows developments in the humanities since the Renaissance (for example, Renaissance architecture, Japanese and Chinese influences on art, the impact of literary and theatrical development during the Renaissance, changes in music including opera and ballet, and major movements in the arts in 19th century Europe)

- content addressed in third grade and in SS.A.5.2.1-8

SS.A.3.2.3 understands the types of laws and government systems that have developed since the Renaissance (for example, the development of democracy, the rise of totalitarian governments and dictatorships, communism, and absolutism)

- content addressed in third grade and in SS.C.1.2.1 and SS.A.4.2.4

SS.A.3.2.4 understands post-Renaissance consequences of exploration that occurred during the Age of Discovery (for example, European colonization in North American and British imperial efforts in India and other countries)

- content addressed in third grade and in United States history (SS.A.4.2.1)

4. **The student understands United States history to 1880.**

SS.A.4.2.1 understands the geographic, economic, political and cultural factors that characterized early exploration of the Americas

- **SS.A.4.2.1.(5.1)** knows selected European explorers and the territories they explored in North America

- **SS.A.4.2.1.(5.2)** understands selected geographical, economical, political, and cultural factors that characterized early exploration of the Americas (for example, impact on Native Americans, war between colonial powers, the institution of slavery)

SS.A.4.2.2 understands why Colonial America was settled in regions

- **SS.A.4.2.2.(5.1)** knows significant events in the colonization of North America, including but not limited to the Jamestown and Plymouth settlements, and the formation of the thirteen original colonies

- **SS.A.4.2.2.(5.2)** understands selected aspects of everyday life in Colonial America (for example, impact of religions, types of work, use of land, leisure activities, relations with Native Americans, slavery)

SS.A.4.2.3 knows significant social and political events that led to and characterized the American Revolution

- **SS.A.4.2.3.(5.1)** understands reasons Americans and those who led them went to war to win independence from England

- **SS.A.4.2.3.(5.2)** knows significant events between 1756 and 1776 that led to the outbreak of the American Revolution (for example, the French and Indian War, the Stamp Act, the Boston Tea Party)

- **SS.A.4.2.3.(5.3)** knows selected aspects of the major military campaigns of the Revolutionary War

- **SS.A.4.2.3.(5.4)** knows reasons why the colonies were able to defeat the British

SS.A.4.2.4 knows significant historical documents and the principal ideas expressed in them (for example, Declaration of Independence, the United States Constitution, and the Bill of Rights)

- **SS.A.4.2.4.(5.1)** knows the history of events and the historic figures responsible for historical documents important to the founding of the United States (for example, the Declaration of Independence, the United States Constitution, the Bill of Rights)

- **SS.A.4.2.4.(5.2)** knows selected principal ideas expressed in significant historical documents important to the founding of the United States (including but not limited to the Declaration of Independence, the United States Constitution, the Bill of Rights, the Federalist papers)

SS.A.4.2.5 understands geographic, economic, and technological features of the growth and change that occurred in America from 1801 to 1861

- **SS.A.4.2.5.(5.1)** understands selected geographic and economic features of the growth and change that occurred in America from 1801 to 1861 (for example, the Lewis and Clark expedition, the Louisiana Purchase)

- **SS.A.4.2.5.(5.2)** understands selected technological developments and their effects that occurred in America from 1801 to 1861 (for example, the cotton gin increasing the need for large numbers of slaves to pick cotton)

SS.A.4.2.6 knows the causes, key events, and effects of the Civil War and Reconstruction

- **SS.A.4.2.6.(5.1)** understands selected economic and philosophical differences between the North and the South prior to the Civil War, including but not limited to the institution of slavery

- **SS.A.4.2.6.(5.2)** knows roles and accomplishments of selected leaders on both sides of the Civil War (for example Abraham Lincoln, Ulysses Grant, Jefferson Davis, Robert E. Lee, Frederick Douglass, William Lloyd Garrison)

- **SS.A.4.2.6.(5.3)** knows causes, selected key events, and effects of the Civil War (for example, major battles, the Emancipation Proclamation, General Lee's surrender at Appomattox Courthouse)

- **SS.A.4.2.6.(5.4)** understands selected aspects of Reconstruction policies and ways they influenced the South after the Civil War

5. **The student understands United States history from 1880 to the present day.**

   SS.A.5.2.1 knows that after the Civil War, massive immigration, big business, and mechanized farming transformed American life

- **SS.A.5.2.1.(5.1)** knows ways American life was transformed socially, economically, and politically after the Civil War (for example, Western settlement, federal policy toward Native Americans, massive immigration, the growth of American cities, big business, mechanized farming)

SS.A.5.2.2 knows the social and political consequences of industrialization and urbanization in the United States after 1880

- **SS.A.5.2.2.(5.1)** knows selected economic, social, and political consequences of industrialization and urbanization in the United States after 1880 (for example, expansion of transportation, development of large population centers, woman's suffrage, rise of organized labor, improvements in the standard of living)

SS.A.5.2.3 knows the political causes and outcomes of World War I

- **SS.A.5.2.3.(5.1)** knows the political causes and outcomes of World War I (for example, isolationism, League of Nations)

SS.A.5.2.4 understands social and cultural transformations of the 1920s and 1930s

- **SS.A.5.2.4(5.1)** understands selected social and cultural transformations of the 1920s and 1930s (for example, impact of the automobile, racial tensions, role of women)

SS.A.5.2.5 understands the social and economic impact of the Great Depression on American society

- **SS.A.5.2.5.(5.1)** understands social and economic impact of the Great Depression on American society (for example, business failures, unemployment, home foreclosures, breadlines)

SS.A.5.2.6 understands the political circumstances leading to the involvement of the United States in World War II and the significant military events and personalities that shaped the course of the war

- **SS.A.5.2.6.(5.1)** understands selected events that led to the involvement of the United States in World War II (for example, German aggression in Eastern Europe, the bombing of Pearl Harbor)

- **SS.A.5.2.6.(5.2)** understands selected causes, key events, people, and effects of World War II (for example, major battles such as the D-Day invasion, the dropping of the atomic bombs on Japan, reasons for the Allied victory, the Holocaust)

SS.A.5.2.7 knows the economic, political and social transformations that have taken place in the United States since World War II

- **SS.A.5.2.7.(5.1)** knows selected economic, political, and social transformations which have taken place in the United States since World War II (for example, Civil Rights movement, role of women, Hispanic immigration, impact of new technologies, exploration of space)

SS.A.5.2.8 knows the political and military aspects of United States foreign relations since World War II

- **SS.A.5.2.8.(5.1)** knows selected political and military aspects of United States foreign relations since World War II (for example, Cold War attempts to contain communism such as in Berlin, Korea, Latin America, and Vietnam; nuclear weapons and the arms race; attempts to secure peace in the Middle East)

6. **The student understands the history of Florida and its people.**

SS.A.6.2.1 understands reasons that immigrants came to Florida and the contributions of immigrants to the state's history

- content addressed in fourth grade

SS.A.6.2.2 understands the influence of geography on the history of Florida

- content addressed in fourth grade

SS.A.6.2.3 knows the significant individuals, events, and social, political, and economic characteristics of different periods in Florida's history

- content addressed in fourth grade

SS.A.6.2.4 understands the perspectives of diverse cultural, ethnic, and economic groups with regard to past and current events in Florida's history

- content addressed in fourth grade

SS.A.6.2.5 knows how various cultures contributed to the unique social, cultural, economic, and political features of Florida

- content addressed in fourth grade

SS.A.6.2.6 understands the cultural, social, and political features of Native American tribes in Florida's history

- content addressed in fourth grade

SS.A.6.2.7 understands the unique historical conditions that influenced the formation of the state and how statehood was granted

- content addressed in fourth grade

B. PEOPLE, PLACES, AND ENVIRONMENTS (Geography)

1. **The student understands the world in spatial terms.**

SS.B.1.2.1 uses maps, globes, charts, graphs, and other geographic tools including map keys and symbols to gather and interpret data and to draw conclusions about physical patterns

- **SS.B.1.2.1.(5.1)** extends and refines use of maps, globes, charts, graphs, and other geographic tools including map keys and symbols to gather and interpret data and to draw conclusions about physical patterns (for example, in the United States)

SS.B.1.2.2 knows how regions are constructed according to physical criteria and human criteria

- **SS.B.1.2.2.(5.1)** knows how regions in the United States are constructed according to physical criteria and human criteria

SS.B.1.2.3 locates and describes the physical and cultural features of major world political regions

- content addressed in third grade

SS.B.1.2.4 knows how changing transportation and communication technology have affected relationships between locations

- content addressed in SS.A.5.2.7

SS.B.1.2.5 knows ways in which people view and relate to places and regions differently

- **SS.B.1.2.5.(5.1)** understands varying perceptions of regions throughout the United States

2. **The student understands the interactions of people and the physical environment.**

SS.B.2.2.1 understands why certain areas of the world are more densely populated than others

- **SS.B.2.2.1.(5.1)** understands reasons certain areas of the United States are more densely populated than others

SS.B.2.2.2 understands how the physical environment supports and constrains human activities

- **SS.B.2.2.2.(5.1)** understands ways the physical environment supports and constrains human activities in the United States

SS.B.2.2.3 understands how human activity affects the physical environment

- **SS.B.2.2.3.(5.1)** understands ways human activity has affected the physical environment in various places and times in the United States

SS.B.2.2.4 understands how factors such as population growth, human migration, improved methods of transportation and communication, and economic development affect the use and conservation of natural resources

- content addressed in SS.B.2.2.3

C. GOVERNMENT AND THE CITIZEN (Civics and Government)

1. **The student understands the structure, function, and purpose of government and how the principles and values of American democracy are reflected in American constitutional government.**

SS.C.1.2.1 identifies the structure and function of local, state, and federal governments under the framework of the Constitution of Florida and the United States

- **SS.C.1.2.1.(5.1)** understands the functions of government under the framework of the United States Constitution

- **SS.C.1.2.1.(5.2)** understands the branches of federal government and their main roles

SS.C.1.2.2 understands the structure, functions, and primary responsibilities of the executive, legislative, and judicial branches of government and understands how all three branches of government promote the common good and protect individual rights

- **SS.C.1.2.2.(5.1)** understands the structure, functions, and primary responsibilities of executive, legislative, and judicial branches of the United States government

- **SS.C.1.2.2.(5.2)** understands ways all three branches of government promote the common good and protect individual rights

SS.C.1.2.3 knows the names of his or her representatives at the local, state, and national levels (for example, city council members, state representatives, and members of Congress) and the name of his or her representatives in the executive branches of government at the local, state, and national levels (for example, mayor, governor, and president)

- **SS.C.1.2.3.(5.1)** knows the names of his or her representatives at the national level (for example, president, members of Congress)

SS.C.1.2.4 knows possible consequences of the absence of government, rules, and laws

- **SS.C.1.2.4.(5.1)** knows possible consequences of the absence of government, rules, and laws

SS.C.1.2.5 knows the basic purposes of government in the United States and knows the basic things governments do in one's school, community, state, and nation

- **SS.C.1.2.5.(5.1)** knows basic things the United States government does in one's school, community, state, and nation

2. **The student understands the role of the citizen in American democracy.**

SS.C.2.2.1 understands the importance of participation through community service, civic improvement, and political activities

- **SS.C.2.2.1.(5.1)** understands the importance of participation through community service, civic improvement, and political activities

SS.C.2.2.2 understands why personal responsibility (for example, taking advantage of the opportunity to be educated) and civic responsibility (for example, obeying the law and respecting the rights of others) are important

- **SS.C.2.2.2.(5.1)** extends and refines understanding of ways personal and civic responsibility are important

SS.C.2.2.3 knows that a citizen is a legally recognized member of the United States who has certain rights and privileges and certain responsibilities (for example, privileges such as the right to vote and hold public office and responsibilities such as respecting the law, voting, paying taxes, and serving on juries)

- **SS.C.2.2.3.(5.1)** knows that a citizen is a legally recognized member of the United States who has certain rights and privileges and certain responsibilities (for example, privileges such as the right to vote and hold public office and responsibilities such as respecting the law, voting, paying taxes, serving on juries)

SS.C.2.2.4 knows examples of the extension of the privileges and responsibilities of citizenship

- **SS.C.2.2.4.(5.1)** knows examples of the extension of the privileges and responsibilities of citizenship

SS.C.2.2.5 knows what constitutes personal, political, and economic rights and why they are important and knows examples of contemporary issues regarding rights

- **SS.C.2.2.5.(5.1)** knows what constitutes personal, political, and economic rights and why they are important (for example, right to vote, assemble, lobby, own property and business)

- **SS.C.2.2.5.(5.2)** knows examples of contemporary issues regarding rights (for example, freedom from discrimination in housing, employment)

D. PRODUCTION, DISTRIBUTION, AND CONSUMPTION (Economics)

1. **The student understands how scarcity requires individuals and institutions to make choices about how to use resources.**

SS.D.1.2.1 understands that all decisions involve opportunity costs and that making effective decisions involves considering the costs and the benefits associated with alternative choices

- **SS.D.1.2.1.(5.1)** knows examples from United States history that demonstrate an understanding that all decisions involve opportunity costs and that making effective decisions involves considering the costs and the benefits associated with alternative choices

SS.D.1.2.2 understands that scarcity of resources requires choices on many levels, from the individual to societal

- **SS.D.1.2.2.(5.1)** understands that scarcity of resources requires choices on many levels, from the individual to societal

SS.D.1.2.3 understands the basic concept of credit

- **SS.D.1.2.3.(5.1)** understands the basic concept of credit

SS.D.1.2.4 understands that any consumer (for example, an individual, a household, or a government) has certain rights

- **SS.D.1.2.4.(5.1)** understands that any consumer has certain rights (for example, an individual, a household, a government)

SS.D.1.2.5 understands the concept of earning income and the basic concept of budget

- **SS.D.1.2.5.(5.1)** creates a simple budget including income and expenses

- **SS.D.1.2.5.(5.2)** knows different ways that money can increase in value through savings and investment (for example, bank savings accounts, stocks, bonds, real estate, other valuable goods)

2. **The student understands the characteristics of different economic systems and institutions.**

    SS.D.2.2.1 understands economic specialization and how specialization generally affects costs, amount of goods and services produced, and interdependence

    - **SS.D.2.2.1.(5.1)** understands economic specialization and how specialization generally affects costs, amount of goods and services produced, and interdependence

    SS.D.2.2.2 understands the roles that money plays in a market economy

    - **SS.D.2.2.2.(5.1)** understands the roles that money plays in a market economy

    SS.D.2.2.3 understands the services that banks and other financial institutions in the economy provide to consumers, savers, borrowers, and businesses

    - **SS.D.2.2.3.(5.1)** understands basic services that banks and other financial institutions in the economy provide to consumers, savers, borrowers, and businesses

    SS.D.2.2.4 knows that the government provides some of the goods and services that we use and that the government pays for the goods and services it provides through taxing and borrowing

    - **SS.D.2.2.4.(5.1)** knows ways the state government provides goods and services through taxation and borrowing (for example, highways and military defense)